Fighting Tactics 8
World Championship Wi[nning]

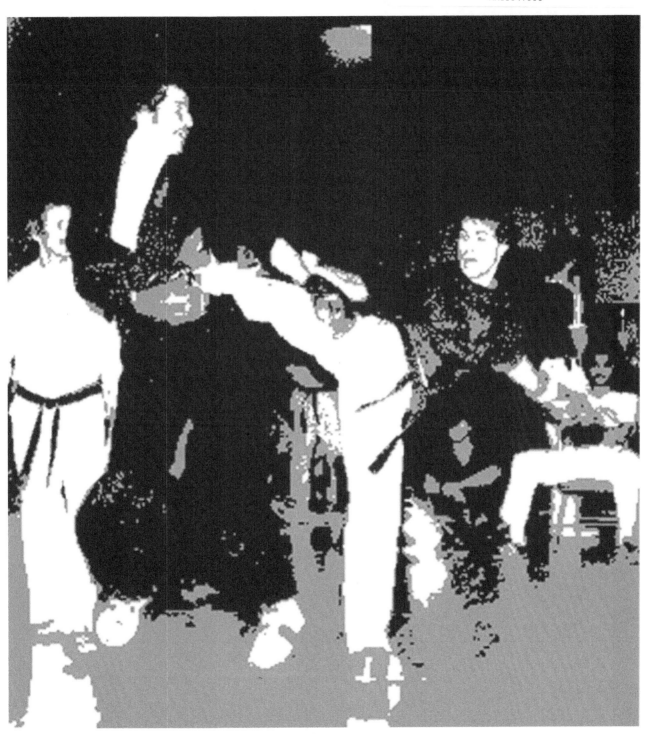

"Super Dan" Anderson

Fighting Tactics & Strategies
World Championship Winning Moves - The American Freestyle Karate Way

by "Super Dan" Anderson
Top Ten National Sparring Champion
FSKA 2002 World Champion

Editor: Dan Anderson
Photography: Mish Handwerker, Tim Gustavson
Featuring: Dan Anderson, Tim Gustavson, Rod Newell
Adobe Acrobat Formating: Mish Handwerker

© 2002, Dan Anderson
All Rights Reserved
Compiled in the United States of America

First Release January 2002

Warning

This book is presented only as a means of preserving a unique aspect of the heritage of Modern Arnis. The author does not make any representation, warranty or guarantee that the techniques described or illustrated in this book will be safe or effective in any self-defense situation or otherwise. You may be injured if you apply or train the techniques illustrated in this book. To minimize the risk of training injury, nothing described or illustrated in this book should be undertaken without personal, expert instruction. In addition, it is essential that you consult a physician regarding whether or not to attempt anything described in this book. Specific self-defense responses illustrated in this book may not be justified in any particular situation in view if all the circumstances or under the applicable federal, state or local law.

Contacting Dan Anderson

Website: http://www.danandersonkarate.com
Postal Mail: P.O. Box 1463 • Gresham, Oregon 97030

Table Of Contents

1. New Forward To The Printed Edition — 1
2. Original Forward — 2
3. The Need For Basics — 6
4. Sparring And Fighting — 6
5. Attitudes Concerning Sparring And Fighting — 7
6. The Situation Dictates The Response — 9
7. Viewpoints In Karate Competition — 9
8. Definition Of Tournament Fighting - The Game — 9
9. Actuality And Apparancy — 11
10. Technical Viewpoints — 14
11. Monitoring — 14
12. Positional Set Up — 20
13. Straight Line Fighting — 25
14. Distancing — 29
15. Angling — 31
16. Timing — 34
17. Faking And Opponent Reactions — 36
18. Simple Moves — 40
19. Complex Moves — 81
20. Sucker Moves — 98
21. Conceptual Aids And Added Information — 117
22. Offensive And Defensive Approach Counters — 117
23. Confronting Drill To Aid Your Sparring — 136
24. Defensive Set Up — 139
25. Responsibility — 140
26. Directional Force — 141
27. Recognition — 143
28. How To Develop New Viewpoints And Skills — 144
29. Directional Focus — 145
30. The First Steps To Learning How To Tournament Fight — 146
31. Doing And Trying — 147
32. More On Operational Modes — 148
33. Desire — 149
34. Afterword — 151

NEW FORWARD TO THE PRINTED EDITION

In October of 2002 I got a call from a long time student of mine, Tom Levak. He wanted me to go to a tournament, *again.* Tom had been after me to compete off and on for years. The tournament

bug never left him and he has been successful, very successful. He has been his age divisional national champion in the USA-NKF (United States of America National Karate Federation) since around 1988. This is the organization which took over the AAU's participation in Japanese type of karate competition in the US.

This tournament, he said was different in two respects. First, the 4th Annual Funakoshi Shotokan Karate Association World Championships was going to be held in Las Vegas and second, it had age divisions - *senior's divisions.* The tournament was going to be held on November 23rd & 24th which meant I had one month to get ready for it. So, I got ready for it. I worked on timing, positioning, straight line fighting and most of all, getting my attitude ready for it. I hadn't competed seriously in 12 years and frankly I had no held over desire to compete again. There was one incentive though. I had never won a world championship. I had been a national champion a number of times but never a world champion. So I worked.

On the day of my competition I was nervous. This was a good thing as in the latter portion of my career, I *couldn't* get nervous. I *couldn't* get into it. This time I could. When my division assembled I was mentally ready but this 50 year old body had a hip that had locked up two weeks before. There went my kicking ability. I spent most of the day watching the rings to see how the calls were being made and stretching out my hip. The judging was excellent and the hip wouldn't budge. My division, the Black Belt age 50-54 was one of the last of the day to be called. When the day was over I had something special to go home with - a world championship

Tom and I with our gold medals

ORIGINAL FORWARD

I have done well for someone who began karate on his 14th birthday of a birthday present. When I first began, it was unusual for someone so young to take karate. Now it is unusual for someone to begin so late. In 35 years , the time sure do change. Here are a few statistics to show you how far a boy from virtually nowhere can come when he sets his mind to it.

- Began karate November 1966. Initial style was Kongsu, a pre-unification Korean style strongly resembling Shotokan.

- Promoted to 1st Degree Black Belt January 1970

- First rated in Karate Illustrated's Top Ten ratings in 1973 after winning Grand Championships in the Western States Karate Championships and Seattle Open Karate Championships and 2nd in Ed Parker's Internationals.

- 1977 - I name my style of Karate "American Freestyle Karate", becoming one of the first styles of American Karate ever.

- 1977 - I became *the only competitor in America* to be rated in both Black Belt magazine and Karate Illustrated magazine's Top Ten fighters of the year.

- Rated in Karate Illustrated's yearbook Top Ten 1977, 1978, 1979 and Sport Karate 1980 in sparring competition.

- Rated in the Top Ten lightweight fighters in the world (Professional Karate Magazine)

- Winner of over 70 Grand Championship titles.

- Rated in the Top Five referees in the US (Karate/Kung Fu Illustrated article).

- Rated in the Top Ten fighters of all time by 7-time national champion Steve Anderson and 3 time national champion Keith Vitali (Karate/Kung Fu Illustrated article).

- Author of a book on Karate sparring, "American Freestyle Karate: A Guide To Sparring", which has been in print and selling all over the world for over 20 years.

- In addition to open style competition, I have won in AAU/WUKO (Japanese organization) events including being one of the only two undefeated American Team members against the Japan National Team (1983 in Cleveland, Ohio), 1984 AAU Nationals Open weight Silver Medallist (sparring), 3 time Oregon State Champion in AAU/WUKO) competition, and double Gold Medallist in the 1990 Seattle Goodwill Games Karate competition (WUKO rules).

- I am also the first heavyweight champion (yes, I had gained some weight) in the International All-Chinese Kung Fu Championships (Vancouver, BC) fighting competition.

- Promoted to 6th Degree Black Belt (Senior Master) in Modern Arnis on June 28, 1992

- Promoted to 7th Degree Black Belt in by the American Teachers Association of the Martial Arts on April 16, 1996.

- Named Instructor of the Year by the World Martial Arts Hall of Fame.

- I have traveled all over the country giving seminars in such diverse places as New York State, Ontario, Canada, Georgia, California, Vancouver, BC, Oregon and Washington.

- I have been featured on the cover of Karate/Kung Fu Illustrated magazine twice and have been featured in every major martial arts magazine in the USA.

As you can tell, I have been busy. You will see in a number of my historical fight photos, me wearing not the traditional karate uniform (gi) but a shirt with a Superman Symbol. There is a story behind this. One of the first articles published of a tournament win, the writer called me "Super Dan" because of my liking for comic books at the time. Seeing this in print infuriated me until at a tournament shortly after that, this guy came up and called me by that nickname...with respect. I ended up being the first competitor to have such a nickname. Many others soon followed until the US tournament karate scene resembled the blues music scene. Nobody was Joe Smith anymore. They were "Smokin' Joe" Smith, "Mad Dog" Joe Smith and so forth.

I have had success teaching over the years and have had a number of students become regional and national successes: Bill Rooklidge, Randy Thomas, Janesa Kruse, Lynn Anderson and Tim Gustavson all made names for themselves and made me proud. Enough of me and my students, here is the book.

This book is the second in the American Freestyle Karate series. There are two types of American Freestyle Karate that I teach. One I teach in my school is the structured format up through Black Belt (which will be available in download book form), much like any style of karate today has. The second is what I teach in seminars or private coaching. This deals with either general principles or specific tactics and strategies that I have come across or formulated over the years. I call these "American Freestyle Karate Principles."

This book deals with techniques and strategies that go into fighting. I have competed in about every type of karate and kung fu competition and feel comfortable in writing a book about this subject.

The main application of these techniques is in a sparring situation. Many of these you can use in a tournament and some of these are only of use in a tournament. A number of these can be adapted to street fighting.

This book is a response to the two questions, "What do I do if..." and "When is the second book coming out?" I've broken the book down into six sections:

Section one has to do with certain aspects of my viewpoint on fighting which need to be taken up and dealt with prior to learning the techniques. Sections two, three and four deal with the techniques themselves. Section five has added information which will aid your overall skill and Section six is basically my sitting down and chatting for awhile about various topics, including my personal selection of a Top Ten of all time.

The techniques in this book are from many sources. I've taken or adapted techniques from #1 fighters to something I saw a 12 year old kid do. If it works, I'll use it. One thing, I've road tested every technique in this book, whether in competition or in the school. I've worked them all.

In my school, there is one thing I strongly stress. It is the difference between only the strong benefiting from Karate training and every student befitting.

This is the practical application of three stages for learning a technique or particular application. I feel one should learn something:

1. Correctly, then
2. Smoothly and then go on to
3. Speedily.

I teach how to learn in those exact steps. It is important that you learn the move and its parts correctly so that you have the mechanics of it down (#1). Then you work on it smoothly without interruptions or jerkiness (#2). Once you can do that, then gradiently begin applying speed and power to it (#3). This way you will find yourself learning in a good step by step progression and won't get lost on the way.

I find that most students are taught with step 2 missing and thereby lose fluid application. Step two is also great for getting a timid student up to where they can confront and handle attacks.

One final note. The original idea of American Freestyle Karate is a concept that has to do with a growth and expansion of knowledge rather than a name of a particular style. I came up with a curriculum in order to instruct students at my school in an orderly manner. The fundamental idea is still there as I come upon approaches to fighting which streamline my own thinking or open up new areas I had not come upon before. Feel free to apply the same to anything in this book. *Take anything you find useful in this book and make it yours - with my blessing.*

Whether in full contact taekwon-do (top left), non-contact point fighting (middle and bottom left), WUKO Japanese style fighting (top right) or open contact point fighting on the national circuit (bottom right), I've played them all...successfully.

THE NEED FOR BASICS

The need for good, sound basics is a must for any martial arts skill. Sound basics are what make a player excel in any sport or field. The primary fact here is that if your basics are in, you can go anywhere. If they aren't, you'll go nowhere.

Since the Bruce Lee movie boom back in the 1970's I've seen kids and others imitate his moves, copy his screams, play with the nunchakus and so forth and then fade away from view. Why? Because unlike his imitators, Lee had his basics in good and solid. He knew balance, timing, power development, fighting principles, coordination - the works. He was so thoroughly grounded in the basics of martial arts that he went way beyond what was the level of expectation and created new standards of excellence. From there he became the single most influential person on the American martial arts scene. All this because he had his basics in.

The very foundation of skill is having your basics in. You can deal with all the flash and dazzle you want but for a long lasting skill and something which will not fade as you grow older, you need good basics. This may not be real to a 20 year old, however, as a former 20 year old champion now in his late 40's it is very real to me. It will be to you as well if you continue in the martial arts for a long time. Besides, all of the flash and dazzle moves have their foundation in basic moves. All of the moves in this book, whether simple or complex, have their roots is simple basic actions. Keep that in mind as you study this book.

SPARRING & FIGHTING

I want to differentiate between these two terms as they are quite different in purpose and application. Sparring is *training* and fighting is *combat*.

SPARRING is where you and a partner work on approaches and tactics to use in fighting. Here is where you try out new techniques or polish up on old ones. When you spar, work on specific actions with specific results or goals to achieve. This way you will get the most out of your sparring time. Sparring is an exercise, just as solo and line drills. The only difference is that it is the closest to the application of something in fighting where the line and solo drills are usually quite structured by your coach/instructor. In sparring you have to have the discipline to structure what you want to work on and then work on it. Use that time wisely. What do you need to work on and polish up? This is the time to do it. This is also the time to cut your partner some slack so that he can work on what he needs, too. Note that I used the term *partner*. You are both working on getting better.

FIGHTING is the application of karate in a win/lose or life/death situation. Your aim is to get him before he gets you, pure and simple. To have an opponent. This relates to the verb, *oppose*, to go against. You have one aim and that is to get him. If he is out to get you, he is opposing you. You have an opponent in a sport match and you have an opponent in a street fight. Note the difference in attitude between sparring and fighting.

Sparring and fighting are two different and distinct actions which might appear the same to an untrained eye. In sparring, more often than not what happens is that a person is somewhere between the two, not really sparring to get better but not really going all out to defeat his opponent, either. It turns out to be a covert one-upsmanship type of affair, which is not very productive in the end, especially for the guy getting beat up. This makes the person getting beat tend to "survival fight" rather than spar. This will lead to bad habits fast.

Use your sparring time to spar and your fighting time to fight. Differentiate between the two so that you can do either one. Oh yeah, make sure that you and your partner have the same agreement when you train so that you both will know whether you're sparring or fighting.

Firing a kick at Chip Wright

ATTITUDES CONCERNING SPARRING & FIGHTING

Here are several attitudes, which I find aid the student of any rank and ability. These pertain to the practice of sparring and fighting.

PREPAREDNESS - You should always be prepared, offensively and defensively. Preparation of offense is fairly natural but defensive preparation and preparation of when your offensive action is cut short (jammed) is usually lacking.

Most people take the "natural reaction" attitude approach to defense. This is fine if you have worked your body and mind over a long period of time to be able to respond with a variety of defensive actions. Then whatever is appropriate, more often than not, will pop up. BUT at the lower ranks and often at black belt level, the natural reaction is some kind of defensive flinch rather than have a workable defense or counter offensive.

The idea here is to be prepared for whatever happens. *Observation* is the key to this. You keep your attention on your opponent as to what he is doing.

Any kind of flinching or blinking will hamper your ability to observe.

If you see his attack or his telegraph at the very beginning, you won't be surprised by it. If you aren't prepared and something goes wrong, you will just stop, even if only for a split second. This can get you hit. Every action, offensive or defensive, should have some kind of back up option for "just in case."

The options will never present themselves unless you train yourself to do them and think that way. When you expect something, it will not surprise you. Preparedness is an attitude that warrants alertness and observation, self observation and observation of your opponent.

DEFINITION - The definition of your technique is directly related to the degree of how prepared you are and how much you intend for the shot to land. Physical definition is clean, sharp technique to a clearly defined target area with no room for slop. Your physical definition sharpens your intention. The form of any technique is set out in such a manner so as to get the maximum benefit from that technique and I'm talking about speed, power, impact, body usage, the whole works. Definition also has to do with balance and weight distribution as well as clean techniques. The greater definition you put into your moves will make your moves stronger, faster and much more effective.

Definition also carries into body movement such as footwork, hip rotation, etc. It is concerned with all aspects of the physical - technique, body position, body alignment, balance, everything. It ties in very directly with preparedness and intention.

INTENTION - Intention is the will power and the drive behind the decision to do something. To drive a technique home to the target, you have to have intention behind it. Intention will give purpose to what you do. You want the technique to go to the target? Make it go to the target! You don't want to get hit? Keep yourself from getting hit!

Intention is actually a simplicity. You don't have to get fancy or serious or anything like that. Just intend to get it done and do it. You do that every day in your life with whatever you accomplish. Anything you have ever done you applied intention do it. Whatever you called it to yourself; want, desire, necessity, it doesn't matter. Apply that same want, desire, necessity to a technique and you will carry it through. I use the term intention as that indicates to me. *Intention is a key factor to driving a technique home.*

These attitudes have a lot to do with your fighting ability becoming a cut above the rest. Preparedness will keep you alert. Definition will enable to hone your body to a fine fighting machine, which will respond with split second timing. Intention is the driving force, which will get the job done. This is a very important trio, isn't it.

THE SITUATION DICTATES THE RESPONSE

Every option has its perfect counter option. Any attack or defense approach can be neutralized by recognition and application of the "correct" opposite which will make it go wrong for him. It is that cut and dried - on paper. Unfortunately, real fighting is anything but that. You don't fight on paper.

There are many intangibles that are thrown into a real fight or sparring situation. The fighter's personalities, emotions, surprises, terrain all play into the situation and response. These are things, which create a live situation instead of a text book case study.

The situation always dictates the response. Where you may run one day, you hit your opponent with a chair the next. This is also true in a sparring match. You may hold your position and hit them one time, you may block and move the next. I found this to be true when I was in competition. I had to fight different opponents of all sizes and weights. Even though this guy was ripe for me to rush forward and hitting him just as he moved, he was too big. I'd get the point but get my head taken off. Pretty uneven exchange for my tastes.

What you do in response depends upon your mental and emotional state right at that exact moment and your physical location (which includes your position in relation to your opponent). These will all play a part in determining how you are going to handle a situation.

You can create a good series of drills by laying out a good number of situations you may have to fight in and then drill them. An example would be if your right arm became immobilized. Practice fighting with your right arm tied behind you. That'll give you a different perspective right there. Or practice in the parking lot. Practice being behind by 2 points and there is only 15 seconds left in the match. You can come up with any number of situations until you become comfortable in any.

VIEWPOINTS IN KARATE COMPETITION

Depending on the region of the U.S. you live in and their rules for competition, most of the techniques in this book can be used for point competition so I'll address the subject of karate point competition here.

What is a viewpoint? A viewpoint is how somebody looks at, feels about and thinks of something. It is a position from where you can view, analyze and handle situations. You can assume all kinds of viewpoints in karate from basic technical to mental to spiritual to gamesmanship. In my first book I use the term "orientation point." Some people like the term "game plan." I find the term *viewpoint* fits it better.

The first viewpoint you can assume for the purpose of competition is that of a game player. This is what tournament karate is - a game. To some it is a very serious game and to others it's a worthless one but it is a game nonetheless. From here we can look at playing the game (fighting a match) from a viewpoint.

One of my game faces was a smile.

One type of viewpoint is to look at from a technical one. Let's say you decide to work your defense from a block and counter viewpoint. Instead of not knowing what you are going to do, that's your strategy. You block and counter as a handle to his attack. That will be a handle to the confusion of "What am I going to do?"

Or your viewpoint can be one of aggressiveness. You look at the other fighter and decide whatever he does is going to be met with aggression. He blinks and you're going forward, firing all guns. There are an infinite number of viewpoints from which to operate from.

You can use any of the offensive or defensive approaches outlined in my first book, anything your instructor teaches, anything you've read about, anything you've come up with yourself, anything. You use a viewpoint to operate out of, base your strategy on and to orient yourself in a moment of confusion. ANY VIEWPOINT IS BETTER THAN NO VIEWPOINT AT ALL.

Most successful fighters combine various viewpoints to suit their own personal approach to fighting. The more skill and experience one has, the more viewpoints one will have at his disposal. You should be able to use or not use any viewpoint that you wish. You should be able to shift viewpoints whenever the situation changes. In any given sparring situation I may go through 5 different viewpoints until I find the worst one for this particular opponent. The entire thrust of this book has to do with the tactics and strategies of sparring and fighting. You can use these to help you in your tournament competition. You can take the initiative by being able to shift viewpoints at a moments notice.

Here's an example: I was up in Canada for a match. For the Grand Championship I was fighting a heavyweight who had less reach than me (very rare I might say). Normally I would stay out of range and pop and pepper my opponent for the points and emerge unscathed. This guy's best action was to go forward very fast and nail him. In other words, he was going to catch me and hammer me unless...I went to him first. Which I did. Every time he moved I went at him. Three rounds and a bloody nose later, I ended up winning the match 11-3.

You seize the initiative by controlling your own actions and responses to any given situation and making your opponent react to you, not you to him.

Read that last line again. This is one of the best kept secrets in any kind of fighting. It is so simple.

You want to one thing but he keeps fouling it up. Instead of going on the mental defensive ("What am I going to do now? What's he going to do?") you shift viewpoints (or I could say tactics - same thing) and keep him on the defensive ("That one's stopped. Let's see what he does with this."). Any time you play the other fighter's game you've lost the initiative. The only exception to this is if you decide you can do this to your own advantage. If you can out punch a puncher or out kick a kicker, go for it. This is what Jose Torres did in his fight for the light heavyweight boxing championship title fight. In the first round, he out jabbed a jab artist. He took his will from him and went on to a 3rd round knock out. You'll notice the key words, YOU DECIDE. You do it because it is your battle plan, not because you can do nothing else. If you're looking into playing the tournament game, the first viewpoint you must assume is one of the game player. In order to do that you must understand the game itself.

DEFINITION OF TOURNAMENT FIGHTING
THE GAME

I was talking to James Haley, a former student and friend of mine, on how to define tournament fighting to a viewing public who didn't have the slightest clue as to what was going on. I was promoting a national tournament with Tom Levak and I was trying to find the simplest way to describe it. James looked at me, smiled and said, "The first person who touches the other one wins." The simplicity of that statement stunned me. How true!

I got around to thinking, with this type of description, how do I elaborate on it but still keep it simple? Well, the better the touch, the more likely it will get called for a point. What are the touches? Karate kicks and punches. What makes it a better touch? The more speed, power and clarity of it. You've got to control it, though. If you touch too hard you'll lose. Where can you touch? Only the target approved areas. These are the basics of tournament fighting.

Tournament fighting, stripped to its barest fundamental premise is a game of, "I get you, you don't get me." or "I get you more times than you get me." It has nothing to do with survival fighting, being a warrior, the all American good sportsman attitude or the virtues of the martial arts although it has been the subject of many heated arguments. When the dust settles, however, you'll find that the guy who touched the other guy the most is the guy who won.

When I say all the above don't get the idea that I don't believe in honor, proper attitude, effective fighting and furthering the positive aspects of the martial arts because believe me, I do. I work very hard at making the art better for others. But I'm talking about the game now and if your don't really see it for what it is, exactly, you're going to set yourself up for hard times playing the game. I was one of the best game players in the history of the game and I know exactly what the tournament game is made up of. Tournament karate is a game of tag, sometimes flaky and sometimes rugged, but a game of tag nonetheless. It itself is not a martial art.

So there is a separation of the two - you have the art and you have the game. If you're going to play the game to win, you've got to get the idea that it is a game with rules and regulations, wins to be gained, losses to be suffered and penalties to be imposed. When you play cards, you know that the ace can count as either 1 or 11 and that may aid you to win. The same goes in karate competition. The game is different from the art and again different from a street fight. When you play the game, know what the game consists of.

ACTUALITY AND APPARANCY

Now let's go over the key hidden point of tournament fighting. If you understand this it'll save you a lot confusion and heartaches. Have you ever sank a good reverse punch in your opponents ribs and stepped back to be utterly amazed that the judges didn't see it. Then your opponent flicks out a backfist that you know wasn't close enough and the flags fly up for his point. Frustrating, isn't it. Let me define two terms:

ACTUALITY - that which really happens.
APPARANCY - that which looks like or appears to have happened.

Apparancy example - this kick is too far away.

Look at the preceding example from these two terms. You sank in the punch. You know it. Your opponent certainly felt it. He even made a face. That is *actuality*, that's what really happened. It didn't get called for a point because the judges didn't see it. Next he flicks out a backfist that he knows didn't get there. The judges called it anyway. That is *apparancy* - it *appeared* to be good enough to the judges to be called a point.

JUDGES SCORE ON APPARANCY, NOT ACTUALITY. They score on what they thought happened, not what really happened. If you understand this one point it will save you a lot of grief. Not all of the time do judges see what actually happened. Judges are people and their reaction times, eyesight, knowledge and so forth are not infallible. Keep that in mind the next time you feel you are being cheated.

The majority of judges I have encountered are very honest, very hard working and want to give each fighter a fair shake. They are usually calling what appears to them to be happening. A number of times they'll call what actually did happen but when they don't, understand why they called what they did.

There is another concept that you need in order to understand the game and how to play it and that is REALITY. Reality is agreement. Along with the written rules of the game there are the unwritten rules as well. Unwritten rules are based on agreement and they make up the reality of the tournament.

Another example from my experience: I was again in Canada fighting in my ring. The rules said light face contact and medium body contact. So that's what I did a number of times. No points. Then I blasted my opponent in the face. Point. I kept this up. My last point I hit him in the face so hard that he stopped in the middle of the ring covering his face. The chief judge went up to him, opened his hands, looked at his nose and said, "It's straight. Point!" I got the point and match. There are the written rules and there are the *ring rules*. It doesn't matter if the written rules say light face contact if ring #3 is allowing for face rearrangement.

The written rules in the example said light face contact but the reality of the ring was hard face contact. You play the rules of that ring and if the rules get changed (enforced) later, you change. The interesting thing is that the game can change from ring to ring in the same tournament. Something I always tell my students is that in a tournament, play the game the way it is given you.

So what is the reality of any given ring? Well, OBSERVE. You'll find out. Here is another thing to observe, the difference between legal techniques and what actually gets called. At any tournament you'll have a number of techniques you are supposed to be able to get a point with. Now take a look and see what gets called the most. In my day it was the reverse punch. In Texas it was the ridge hand. Observe. You'll see what the judges like and then if you throw it, it'll more often get called.

When you play the game, keep in mind what I said about APPARANCY and ACTUALITY and what gets called for a point is apparancy. Also find out what the REALITY of the situation by observing what gets called and what doesn't. That will get you farther in the game than anything.

Receiving an award for the Northwest Outstanding Karate-ka 1973

TECHNICAL VIEWPOINTS

This section has to do with preparation for the techniques you will learn in the following sections. These have to do with monitoring, movement, distancing, timing and so on, which are very important in doing the techniques themselves.

MONITORING

I went over a lot on the subject of monitoring in my first book but for those who do not have a copy of it, I have included it here. Monitoring is my way of describing my method of *attack recognition*. What I have my students do is to watch the attacking agents, the hand. I feel this is the safest portion of the opponent to watch. There are many schools of thought concerning this. Some watch the eyes, some watch the chest, some watch the shoulders. I feel watching the hands is the best. If you tilt your head slightly forward your range of vision will cover from the hands to the thighs. This will cover spotting any telegraph of any kick or punch your opponent will throw.

Here are the technical aspects to monitoring. There are three parts to an attack:
1. point of origin, 2. travel route and 3. point of destination. When you watch the hands you have your eyes on point 1, the origin point. When they move you see it immediately.

The *positional center line* is a vertical straight line that cuts the body in half, side to side.

Front facing   *Angle facing*   *Side facing*

Example of three points to an attack using a back fist (left series) and side kick (right series)- photo one point of origin, photos two and three travel route, photo four destination.

When you monitor your opponent's hands, you spot their *initial movement* in conjunction with the positional center line. They will either cross it (backfist), move away from it (ridge hand, hook punch) or go straight with it (jab, straight punch). When you watch your opponent's hands and where they go as regards the positional center line, you will be able to recognize the telegraph of the type of punch they will throw. You can tell in the first 4 inches the travel route of the punch.

Back fist - The hand moves across the center line.

Ridge hand - The hand first moves away from the center line.

Straight punch - The hand neither crosses or moves away from the center line.

How can you tell if a kick is coming if you're watching the hands? Bend your head forward a bit. This way, when you watch the hands, you will have the hands in the top range of your vision. His thighs will be in the bottom range of your vision.

If your head is erect, you'll miss the thighs. Bend your head forward. Catch the hands and thighs.

You will see the thighs move upwards to position for a kick. You will easily see the foot at the end of the leg. The way the foot is positioned for a particular kick will tell you which kick your opponent is set up for. The foot moving away from the center line will either be a round or hook kick, depending on which side it goes. If the body is sideways and the foot is exactly on the center line, it'll usually be a side kick. If the body is forwards and the foot is on the center line, it'll be a front kick.

In the front kick, the leg is on either side of the center line

See how the position of the lead foot can telegraph which kick your opponent will throw. The next series is presented top to bottom showing how the direction of the point of the lead foot can show you how your opponent is set up for a round, side or hook kick.

Round kick and hook kick travel away from the center line. Side kick comes straight up the center line.

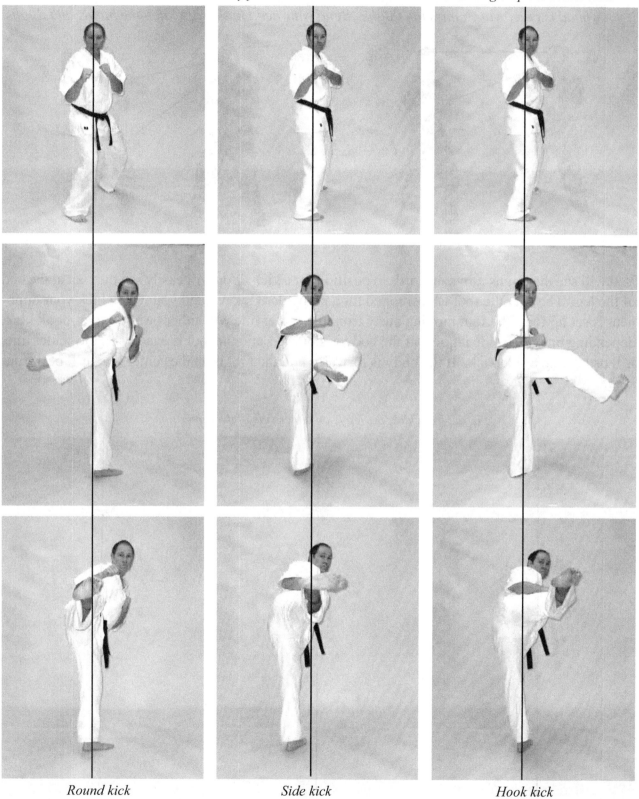

Round kick *Side kick* *Hook kick*

I will tell you why I am so certain of these telegraphs. A fighter will set himself up to throw a technique from the easiest position to throw it from. *In other words, a person will not try to make it hard for himself.* Test out for yourself. Put your forward leg in a toes facing forward position. What is the easiest kick to throw from there? Front kick, round kick, side kick or hook kick? That is an easy one. Now test the same for which kick from each of these positions: toes at a 45 degree angle, foot totally sideways, toes slightly turned inwards from a sideways position (pigeon toed). You'll find that there is one kick for each position that is the easiest for that position.

Go back and look at the foot positions in the last series of photos. Later, in your sparring, check it out. This will help greatly for spotting a kick telegraph.

Like I said there are different methods of watching for telegraphs. I'll outline my disagreements with watching some of them. I don't watch the eyes because the eyes can't come out of the skull and hit me. Eyes can't hurt me. I've received some evil looks before and I'm still here. I'll look at the eyes briefly to read how my opponent feels. Is he scared, angry, crazy? The eyes will tell me that but not much else. Your opponent might look at his intended target before he hits and then again he might look one place and hit another. For fighting, for me, the eyes are too unreliable.

I don't watch the chest is that watching the chest comes from boxing, *a shirt off sport*. If the shirt is off you can see the muscles flex prior to a strike if your opponent is developed enough for the flex to be seen. Most people wear shirts, though, so I don't find it very reliable. The same with karate people. They wear jackets. It's hard to see the muscles flex through the jacket.

I don't watch the shoulders because although the shoulders will telegraph motion, they won't telegraph *the actual attack*. Watching the shoulders isn't quite precise enough for me to rely on. I will watch the shoulders if I'm going to use defensive angling. More on that later.

I watch the attacking agent. This has been the most effective method of attack recognition I have experienced and it has been effective for everyone I have taught it to. Make sure that if you adopt it that you see the hands in the top range of your vision, as in the diagram, so that you can see the thigh in to lower range. This way you can spot all of your opponent's attacks, the real ones and the fakes. Speaking of fakes, after using this method for awhile, you'll be able to spot when they try to fake with ease.

POSITIONAL SET UP

Positional set up has to do with how your opponent is set up. This is a prediction tool. How your opponent is set up will tell you what he is most likely to throw. When I teach this concept at seminars I make an example of its efficiency by sparring several members of the seminar, predicting what my partner will do in advance to someone who is standing off to the side. I'll square off with him, stop before any action is done, go off to the side and tell a different person (whispering) what I expect my partner to do and then go back and spar the person. I have always been 70-98% accurate. Anytime you can tell that much what your opponent is going to do, you have quite an advantage.

1) WEIGHT DISTRIBUTION - Most fighters have a way of tipping you off as to whether they are offensive, defensive or neutral. This is whether their weight is more on the front foot, rear foot or balanced 50-50. An offensive fighter is usually weight forward. A defensive fighter usually has their weight more towards the rear leg and a balanced fighter is usually 50-50.

Weight distribution is fairly reliable but against experienced fighters, it's the one I find the least reliable. An experienced fighter can use any weight distribution and mask his real intentions. He might rest his weight backwards to throw a lead leg kick, for example. Against less experienced fighters or fighters who are set in their ways, I find this useful. The nice about watching weight distribution is that a lot of fighters do not watch closely their own weight distribution so they present you with a tip of what they're going to do.

Top photo - Weight forward = offensively set up
Middle photo - Weight backward = defensively set up
Bottom photo - Weight evenly distributed = can go either way

2) DISTANCE BETWEEN THE FEET - The distance between the feet of your opponent is a very good clue as to whether he is going to kick with his front foot or not. Here I am talking about his initial move, *his kicking with the front foot* without any other type of pre-kick preparation. If his feet are about one to one and a quarter shoulder width apart, count on the kick coming.

Note in the above photos the feet are a short distance apart making a lunge kick easy to do.

If his feet are wider than that, look for a step first or the rear leg kick. If his feet are wider than one and a quarter shoulder width he'll *need* some sort of step first to front leg kick. I'm talking about offensive kicking. A defensive kick can come out of a wider stance but the weight distribution will be towards the rear leg.

Note that in the above photos the feet are spread apart necessitating a step prior to kicking.

Check it out. Put you feet in a short stance and then lead leg kick. Pretty easy. Now do it out of a deep stance without footwork set up. Good luck. See how the body goes off balance by comparison? If this happens to your body, it'll happen to another's just the same. I find that the front leg lunge kick is limited to about a shoulder and a quarter width stance.

3) HAND AND FOOT POSITION IN RELATIONSHIP TO THE POSITIONAL CENTER LINE. This is a very slick one. Remember the previous section on Monitoring? This is the use of how to read telegraphs by how your opponent holds his hands. If he moves his hand away from the centerline, it's coming back at you in a hook or angle type strike. If it crosses the centerline, it's coming at you in a backhand fashion. If it just runs parallel to the centerline, it'll be straight at you.

How he holds his hands in regards to the centerline will tell you what he wants to throw.

A lot of karate fighters hold the lead hand across the centerline. What's coming then? Backfist, of course. Take a look at your opponent's hand position. Are they up in a boxers position? Which way do the "guns" face? From watching how your opponent sets his hands up in the first you'll see what he can throw from where he is before *he* even knows it. That is a nice advantage. Also, does he only have one of his hands aimed at you? One handed fighters will do that. One will be pointed and the other will be off. The pointed one is the live one.

Back fist set up   *Straight punch set up*   *Hook punch set up*

4) POINT POSITION OF THE FEET - If you know anatomy and the natural function of body parts this is a dead give away. Your foot and ankle and knee and hip are connected. None move independently of the other. You can rotate the foot a tiny bit but not much. As you turn the foot, *you'll turn the shin, knee, thigh and hip as well.* The leg functions as a unit. If you bend your leg, pick it up and straighten it you will see what the leg naturally does. Do the drill from the section in Monitoring and see if I'm right.

If the foot is pointed forwards the easiest kick will be front kick. If the foot is pointed inward at an angle the easiest kick will be an angle or round kick. If the foot is pointed exactly sideways the easiest kick, for most, will be the side kick. Pigeon toe the lead foot and you'll find that hook kick is the usual kick. The point of the lead foot is also based on this premise: *a fighter will never make things hard for himself to do.* That is totally backwards of the aim of any endeavor. You don't learn and perfect something so that you will continue to have trouble with it. That is so simple yet it is overlooked in many areas. Why worry about what kick or punch your opponent is going to throw? He is telling you in his body position. He might as well write you a letter and mail you a check. If you learn how to read his position it is that easy.

When the front foot faces forward, the easiest kick to throw is the front kick with the forward or back leg

Setting up your opponent for a front leg counter using the front kick

Following up on a fake with the rear leg front kick

Looking at the above photos, you can tell I am set up for the front kick by the point of my feet.

The point of the foot at an angle and the bend of the knee sets up the leg to be thrown in a round kick fashion

With the front foot pointing at an angle, the easiest kick to do is a round type of kick.

When the edge of the foot is pointing towards the opponent, the leg is set up for either side or hook kick.

Side kick (sequence on left) or hook kick (sequence on right)

Positional Set up is one of the best methods of immediate orientation in a sparring or fighting situation that I know of. At the beginning you may not have an opportunity to feel out your opponent so if you know positional set up, you'll be ready anyway. Develop the skill of being able to do a quick scan of your opponent's position and check the following points above.

When you can do this you're ready for the next step. This is the monitoring of yourself. From a particular position, what is the easiest technique to throw from there? Second best? Third best? Figure that out so that you don't try to fire a technique from a position which doesn't suit it, like a front kick from a side position and so on. Once you've done that you now combine knowing your position and his position. If you are looking at offensively, is your opponent in a position *to be hit by your technique?* This is very important. You might be set up to throw a backfist but if his lead hand is up high, the target is taken away from you. So what do you do, throw the backfist anyway? If you do you're wasting motion and setting yourself up to get hit.

Different positions and different placements will yield different target options. Get to where you can recognize your opponent's position and your own position and what can be done from each. Can you go right from where you are or do you have to maneuver him into a better position? Or do you have to change your own position to get a different target? Take each point, one at a time, and become proficient at observation of your opponent and then yourself. Surprisingly enough, your opponent will tell you exactly what he wants to do...if you know how to read what his body is saying.

STRAIGHT LINE FIGHTING

Nearly everyone fights in a straight line pattern, movement being forward and back. I want to present a particular concept of straight line fighting and a method which may aid you in developing it.

Straight line fighting is typified by two main points: 1) going from point A to B (you to him) as fast as possible and 2) doing so with disregard to peripheral or outside distraction. A peripheral or outside distraction, in this application, is any attack which doesn't come directly at you.

Look at the idea of a Japanese fighter. This is a specific attitude. A Japanese fighter fights with the samurai attitude of "You cut my flesh, I cut your bone." If you have ever seen a samurai movie where the two fighters square off, come in at the same time and the fighter with the better timing

cuts a hair sooner than his opponent and kills him, you got the idea. This epitomizes the idea of straight line fighting and disregarding peripheral distractions. He will get to a certain distance from you and then 100% total commitment to get the attack through.

It is a commonly agreed upon principle that a straight line can beat a curve. Example: a straight punch will reach the target before a hook punch because of the directness of it. Here is where the samurai attitude comes in. You go straight in, cutting any action of his short by taking the shortest possible route. You may get clipped (You cut my flesh...) but he'll get drilled (I cut your bone). This type of attitude must be there or else the physical mechanics won't work to 100% optimum functioning.

I'll give you the example of how I developed it for myself. In May, 1982, I planned on entering a W.U.K.O. (World Union Karate-do Organization) rules tournament. W.U.K.O. rules then were very Japanese style oriented and were very different than the open rules I was used to. Open tournaments allow for all sorts of techniques and Japanese tournaments concentrate on front kicks and straight punches. I thought it would be fun if I, an open rules fighter, won a Japanese rules tournament.

So, I got to work on my attitude. I concentrated on three things; 1) straight line, 2) no hesitation and 3) samurai attitude. The key thing here is that I was not pretending with my attitude. I was taking that particular attitude and making that mine. It was me. That was how much I worked on the attitude.

My students couldn't understand it. I was sparring with an approach that was so simple that they should've been able to pick me apart with all sorts of moves and couldn't. I then went to the tournament and amazed everyone...but me. I ended up winning my weight division and the open weight (all weights) as well. I beat fighters who had grown up in the Japanese system including the U.S. heavyweight champion. Since then I fought and won in a number of Japanese tournaments including getting two gold medals in the 1990 Goodwill Games (at the ripe old age of 37). The main point of this story is that it all began with my taking on the attitude described earlier and getting into it to such a degree that it became *my own attitude* with nothing artificial about it.

One nice thing about my being an open stylist was that it aided me in that I have seen all sorts of techniques thrown at me from all angles. I was not going to get hit by anything unexpected so the surprise factor was way down. After training like this my respect for this type of attitude increased greatly. The attitude of going straight in without hesitation is one of the strongest I have come up against and is valuable in overall training.

My own development of the approach went like this: I went on the basis that if an attack didn't come down on the Positional Center Line, I disregarded it. The Positional Center Line is described in the preceding section on Monitoring. Make that line about three inches thick and if the attack doesn't come down it, disregard it, move in and blast away. To make this work you need to have 1) no hesitation. If you hesitate he can get you. 2) Move your body down that space as if your body *fit in* that small of a space. If you do this with these two points in mind, you won't believe how sharp and straight to the point your action will be.

This is how I viewed my opponent. If anything didn't come down the three inch strip (illustrated by the clarity of that portion of the photo) it was disregarded and I went straight forward.

Example of straightlining a round kick, going inside the curve.

Example of straightlining a back fist. It isn't coming down the 3 inch line so I ignore it.

Using the straight line approach against Eddie Newman. This was at the Top Ten National Karate Championships in Los Angeles in 1979. Bill Wallace is refereeing.

A good way to use the above description is to imagine it. Mock it up and imagine yourself moving inside that 3 inch line, going inside or round kicks, ridge hands, backfists and spin kicks. Picture yourself beating to the punch front kicks and straight punches hitting them right as they move. Razor sharp reflexes, that's what you want to imagine.

With this type of approach the only thing you'll have to watch out for is running into an attack that is coming straight at you like a straight punch, side kick or a high chambered front kick. It would be like running into an outstretched spear. Keep your eyes open when you do this but especially keep your attitude strong. Remember, I made this work for me so you can do the same.

DISTANCING

Distance is the amount of space between you and your opponent. For each opponent there will be a very specific distance from them that will be optimum for you. Most people look at distance from an offensive point of view. "How close do I have to be to be able to get him?" That makes one distance of yours for each opponent. Well, if each opponent had the exact same reach, perhaps that would be all right. But opponents come in all different sizes and some can out reach you so my idea of distancing is defensive rather than offensive based.

Mine is based on *your opponent's* effective hitting range. I said your opponent's hitting range, not yours. *What is the farthest distance away from you can he be and still tag you (not hit you solidly) with the least amount of telegraph (seeable move) motion?* That will establish the distance you want to fight from. This is what I call the Critical Distance Line (CDL).

Establishing a CDL against a long range opponent. He can touch but not hurt.

Establishing a CDL against a shorter ranged opponent

If you're inside the critical distance line you'll be too easily hit. If you're too far outside it, it'll take you too long to cross the distance to hit effectively. You want to be on the outside edge of that line. That creates your safety zone.

Here I am too close to my opponent. He can reach out and hit me without stepping.

You have to establish a CDL *for each* opponent as each opponent differs in effective hitting range, even if only a little. The easiest way to establish this safety zone is to go by what your opponent's reach with the rear leg front kick is. You visibly measure that distance from his hip to the floor. This is a safe method of establishing range as the legs are the longest reaching weapon and the front kick is the strongest, least telegraphed weapon. One person at 6 feet tall might have a different leg length than another person at the same height.

Here's a good example using two of my Black Belts. Tom Levak is all torso and short legs while Bill Rooklidge has legs almost up to his neck. They're about the same height. I'd never get as close to Bill as I would Tom. He'd kick me to death. The same is for my partners in the photos. Tim Gustavson has legs from here to New York while Rod Newell's range is just "next door." Check it out with students from your school. You'll find that it is true what I say about range.

Some of my students were having a difficulty with the concept of critical distance so I came up with a humorous way of looking at it. What is the closest you can to be to someone and insult him? That can be your *Critical* Distance Line. You don't want to be so close that when you say, "Hey stupid!" you get a fist in your face. That bit of humor registered with them and they got the point.

Once you know and can apply distancing to your advantage, you can manipulate it as well. I have a saying in my school, *"If you know the rule, you can cheat on the rule."* If you find that someone doesn't know CDL, you can use their lack of knowledge by creeping inside of the CDL. Then you get too close before he even knows you're too close.

Distancing has been one of my greatest weapons in my career. It will do you well to make a good study of it.

ANGLING

The purpose of angling is to move yourself from a position your opponent could hit you in to one which is harder for him to hit you in. That's pretty simple. If your are straight in-line with your opponents ability to move forward, you are easy to hit. If you move off of that straight line to one on an angle and then you become not so easy to hit.

I discussed in a previous chapter Straight Line Fighting which, direction wise, is in a forward manner. Angling is moving in any direction which is off that straight line.

One thing you can always count on is that your opponent will set you up for him to hit your from a position which is *easy for him* to move from. He will set himself up in his best position to attack you from. He will not make it hard for himself. That you can bet money on. I have never fought anyone who purposely faced me in a position that they felt was weak. That's why I said when you angle you put yourself in a position that is harder for him to hit you from. Usually he will readjust himself to get back into his position. When he does that you can either hit him during the readjustment or angle again as he readjusts. Either way *you are denying him his position.* This is a good way to gain the upper hand.

With defensive angling you would angle off their straight line approach just as they *begin to move*. Not as they begin to attack. By the time you recognize the attack, you might be hit. As he begins to move. That's when you angle. With offensive angling you would take the initiative and angle off the straight line approach and hit him from a different direction. You could hit him flat footed or as he readjusts.

Angling was introduced to the American tournament scene by all time great, Joe Lewis and was perfected by three time number one player, Keith Vitali. All of the angling done in the U.S. in tournaments are basically offshoots of Joe Lewis or Keith Vitali.

There are two prerequisites to skilled angling and they are *distancing* and *mobility*. If you are going to use movement for defense you need room to move in. If you are too close you will get hit before you can, yourself, move. It's that simple. The earlier chapter on distancing lays out my idea of safe distance from your opponent.

Let's take distancing into consideration first. When you are on the Critical Distance Line, your opponent will have to execute a large motion to get to you. He will have to move his whole body. He won't be able to lean in and hit you. He'll have to step. This is what you want. *You move when his shoulders show the first sign of movement.* That's the timing point. Not when you recognize that he has committed to his entry. That is way too late. When his shoulders *start to move*.

You have this datum to operate on: ANYTHING THAT TAKES MORE MOTION TO EXECUTE WILL TAKE MORE TIME TO EXECUTE IT IN.

This is a very important part of angling. Your chances of success angling against a large motion will be greater than a small motion. The greater your distance between you and your opponent will give you more time to do your angle.

Angle stepping - You can roll your shoulder either way depending on the counter attack you use

Stepping towards the forward shoulder and countering a kick

Stepping towards the forward shoulder and countering a punch

There is a second part to defensive angling, angling the upper body. You use this when you are too close to step away. When you angle the upper body you should still be close enough to counter attack. Don't be so turned or twisted that your counter has no power. You want to hit him as you angle. If you don't you are still close enough to get hit by him. When you angle you can also go into a clinch or takedown and grapple as well.

Example of angling the upper body (without stepping) and countering a reverse punch

The key point I want to get across pertaining to defensive angling is to get off his straight line approach to you. It's like a train coming down the tracks at you. You need to get off the tracks - all the way off the tracks. If you leave your foot on the tracks, what happens to your foot? It gets sliced. Work your angling as if you are on the tracks and you'll move enough and fast.

TIMING

Timing is one of the most misunderstood concepts people have. At seminars I will ask students, "What is timing?" I will get as many different answers as the number of people I ask. I never get the same answer whether from white or black belts. Everyone has a feel for it but never can seem to articulate it. Well, if it isn't defined, it isn't understood. Here is my working definition of timing:

TIMING IS A DECISION OF WHEN.

When what? When anything. "When" has to do with the exact moment you do/say/think/start/stop anything. Exact moment exactly delineated. So if you are going by exact moment, you'll find that the errors in timing are not based in speed. You didn't go too fast or too slow. *You went too early or too late.* Too early, too late. Those correspond with an exact moment. My favorite example I give to students has to do with going to the bathroom. If you get there too early, I hope you have a magazine. If you get there too late, I hope you have a change of clothes. If you get there at the right moment, life is good. Perhaps not the most tasteful of examples but certainly one that we all have reality on.

If you can go before, in between or at the end of your opponent's action, you can catch him at a disadvantage. Before, during, at the end of; these are all "whens," exact moments. To develop how to use these "whens," you start on slow timing drills, some that do not need a fast recognition skill on your part. You do it at an easy speed and an easy to do drill. I'll go over one in a moment. Then, as you progress, you can do faster and faster drills until your timing is split second precise. Then you can spar using the drills. Illustrated below are examples of different "whens."

In the first example, you are hitting before your opponent comes at you. Most people aren't totally ready to take off. Often they'll bend their legs prior to actually attacking. When you see their shoulders drop (indicating the knee bend) that's when you attack. You'll catch him off guard.

In this example you are timing your strike in between your opponent's strikes. He does a front kick. You time your entry and attack as the kick retracts, before he can fire another attack.

Here you're timing your attack when your opponent is done attacking.

Here are two simple but effective timing drills. Your move is to step in and backfist right when (*as, not after*) your partner drops his arm. See? Simple. Another good one is to watch an action movie on television while being in a stance. The scene changes, you attack. Or you retreat. The exact moment of change, bing - you go. If you watch a soap opera you'll end up standing around for awhile until the scene changes. You can create any drill which hinges on an exact moment when you have to move.

OFFENSIVE TIMING - The key point to offensive timing is to go on a point of change. Any point of change will do. When a person changes from one thing to another, he will have some attention on what he is doing. It won't matter if it's the least bit of attention. Any attention on what he is doing is that much attention *off of you*. That is the time you attack.

This change or shift of position can be in the form of stance change, going forward, going backward, weight shift, an advance, a retreat, when he comes to a halt, etc. All you need is an instant of his *starting* to do something different than what he was doing. He shifts, you go. The action movie on television drill is a good one to develop this. Keep in mind that your offensive timing will have greater success if you time your offense as he *starts to change*.

DEFENSIVE TIMING - In defensive timing you are also watching for a change in your opponent. The thing you are looking for is telegraph of motion. When your opponent shows you, through body language, that he is preparing for or starting an attack, you go into your defensive motion. His knees bending shows you he is preparing to take off on you. His shoulders moving will telegraph motion towards you. His hand or thigh movement will telegraph the attack.

You will have four basic defensive options: 1) get out of the way of the attack, 2) block the attack, 3) hit him as he starts to come in to attack or 4) hit him in between attacks. The last one is especially tricky as your distancing has to be sharp as well. If you are going to use a block, you will need to do what I call "touch trigger." Your touch on the block is what sets your counter into action, just like the trigger fires the bullet.

If you hit your opponent just as he begins to move you need to recognize his beginning motion. Here is where I watch the shoulders. Before his body can come at you, his shoulders will move. It doesn't matter what kind of move - up, down, forward, they'll move.

Defensive Jumping punch on Al Francis of Texas at the US Championships in Dallas, 1974.

Timing is a decision of when. Learn how to recognize "what" (covered in Monitoring) and you will be able to develop the "when."

FAKING AND OPPONENT REACTIONS

Since there are many techniques in this book which use fakes to set up your opponent, I had better go over the subject a bit. What is a fake? *A fake is something that looks like it is coming but it isn't.* You'll notice that I didn't say it was a false technique or entry. That is the critical point of a fake. It is an *unfinished* technique or entry *that is cut short by your opponent's reaction.* Most people wonder why their opponent doesn't react to his fake. He's probably doing a half way motion. A person won't react to something he doesn't feel is real.

How do you tell what kind of fake your opponent will react to? I made a major breakthrough by examining a continuing dilemma of mine when sparring Fred King. He would use "leading center" fakes (head, shoulder and hip fakes) on me and I would use "technique fakes" on him. I couldn't make him flinch and I wondered why he was flicking his shoulder or hip at me when I could tell he wasn't firing at me. Then one day it hit me out of the blue. The reason our fakes didn't work on each other is because *neither of us were trained in the other's way of thinking.* I was not taught the theory of leading centers and he wasn't taught to watch techniques. As far as I was concerned he was just jerking his body and that meant nothing to me. He never fell for my technique fake because he could tell by my shoulders that I was not committing to the attack.

This lead to the breakthrough and the why of failed faking. YOUR FAKING MUST PARALLEL THE EDUCATION OF YOUR OPPONENT. Fascinating. I then figured out how to safely test how your opponent has been educated and the funny thing of it is that he never figures out that you are setting him up. I've found three predominant ways of faking. Most fighters will fall for at least one of them.

I have found that your opponent will usually respond to a *commitment, shoulder or hip lead or a technique.* When I test my opponent for what he'll fall for, I check these three, in this exact order. This is the safest for me as each one I have to get closer to him to work the fake. You never know what your opponent has been educated into or out of. An interesting side note here is I've found that an untrained person will react to techniques very easily. The funny thing is that a student can be educated out of one kind of reaction right into another. The trick is finding out what your opponent has been educated into and then using that.

Before you think I am trying to tell you that any instructor will teach a student to fall for a fake let me clarify something. An instructor will teach a student a way of reading what his opponent is going to do. He'll tell them to watch the shoulders for movement or the committed entry or the actual attack. "When your opponent _____, defend yourself." What kind of telegraph is your looking for? That is what you are testing. Is he looking for you to commit? To telegraph your attack by moving your shoulders or hips? To fire a technique? *That* is what you test.

COMMITMENT FAKE - This is where your opponent watches for committed entries. Are you coming or not? You take off with a short distance burst and see if your opponent responds. If he flinches or freezes, you've got it. If he fires and cuts it short because you didn't fully come in, you've got it. If he's calm or doesn't respond, abandon it. Offensive reverse punch #5 in the technique section is a good example of this.

LEADING CENTERS - The idea of leading centers is that you watch the head, shoulders or hips for telltale movement of a technique. Before your opponent can cross the distance to you, his shoulders and hips will have to move first. Before a kick or punch is fired, the hips or shoulders will usually move first. This is what is meant by leading centers.

TECHNIQUE FAKE - This is where you do a technique, full commitment, and then cut it off *as* you get a reaction. The key point is that you just don't "fake." You don't think of this as a false action or a "not-do." This is the real thing, firing at them and as he reacts, you hit in the opening.

The way I test someone is I'll check commitment, leading centers and techniques, in that order. A commitment fake you don't need to get into range of your opponent. You "pump" him with a beginning of an entry step and see if he reacts. If he doesn't then I'll pop a hip fake (looking like a kick is coming in) or a shoulder fake (looking like some kind of punch is coming in) and see if he reacts. If no reaction then I'll fake a technique of some sort. That'll usually do it. If none of the above doesn't get any reaction, then I just attack or try something else. It's rare that I don't get a reaction, though.

Commitment fake - You burst forward but only 3-4 inches. Make it a very fast in and out action. Pop your shoulder forward as you do this. This will give the impression of your attacking. Watch to see if he flinches. If he does, the next time you only do the "in" of the in-out. Follow up forward with your attack. The short-long step in the Simple Moves section of the book illustrate this.

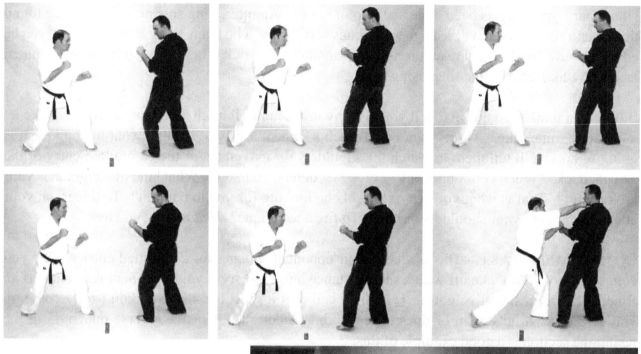

Using the fake and follow up to attack Jim Dolmadge, a good training buddy, in a match Grants Pass, Oregon Neither of us let our friendship stand in the way of a good match.

Leading Center fake - I pop my shoulder upward to get his attention upwards and then low kick.

Technique fake - Step forward and throw a partial low punch and as he reacts, kick to the face

Again, what I do is test each of these fakes, a commitment fake, a leading center fake and a technique fake *in that precise order* to see what my opponent will fall for. I find this to be the safest way to see how my opponent has been educated.

SIMPLE MOVES

Simple moves are moves that do not require that your opponent reacts in an extremely specific way for the technique to work. You just execute the move. Simple moves depend on 1) precision - precision range, timing, technique and judgment and 2) commitment. A simple move need not be a single move. A simple move may contain a couple of different attacks or fakes in it.

The primary requirement is that it can be executed with a minimum of need for optimum conditions. If you're relying on your opponent to shift 87% of his weight backwards, drop his right hand, turn his body away and worry about if he has his next months rent, you don't have a simple move. It's a complex move and it will be covered in the next chapter.

Often a simple move is the best. How many times have you seen a fighter seem to just reach out and hit his opponent? It looks like there was nothing to it. He stood there and smack! End of story. You see this happen a couple more times and it looks like he has a duck for an opponent. Or he's Superman. Neither is quite true. What happened was the application of a true skill. You'd seen simplicity in action.

There is an American attitude of "complexity = skill." Although the mechanical ability to execute a difficult move is nice to have, don't overlook the simple move. Getting stuck into only attempting the slick move will get you into trouble fast when fighting someone who is experienced. The best mixture for a fighter is a mixture of simple, complex and sucker moves so that you won't be just one kind of fighter. Each type will be covered in the following chapters. Some of these moves are fine for fighting and some are tournament moves only. They have all been "road tested." Here are a number of simple moves which I have found to work.

Fight photo first published in Black Belt magazine.
This is from the 1971 Western States Karate Championships grand title match against Bob Barrow.

THE REVERSE PUNCH

The reverse punch is a straight punch thrown off of the rear side. The term comes from an inaccurate translation of the Japanese term, "gyaku tsuki." Gyaku is "opposite" which makes sense when you think of the opposite side of the lead side. I couldn't make sense of what the reverse in reverse punch was for the longest time. You didn't punch behind yourself. Anyway, the reverse punch is the most widely used technique in karate and the most called one in tournaments. For whatever reason it is the most agreed on technique for scoring. It is like the straight right in boxing. It carries a wallop. There are many ways to get this punch through. Here are several. A number of these are named after the person I got them from.

THE TOM LEVAK SPECIAL

Tom Levak is a student of mine who delights in training in all kinds of sports these days except for karate. He runs, skis, swims, lifts weights and so forth but I haven't seen him in the school for years. He loves to compete, however, and does quite well at it. In AAU competition he has been the US Seniors 55 and over champion for the last 5 years. At the time of this writing he is 60 and I wouldn't be surprised if he ends up being the "100 and over champion."

His best move is to get his opponent to react to a backfist that never comes because he never threw it. It is a very simple set up and funny one, at that. He places his guard as in the first photo. As he comes in he rotates his torso upward in a 45 degree angle while keeping the lead arm glued in the shoulder socket. This rotation action will approximate a lead backfist *just enough* to get a reaction. You fire the reverse punch in the opening.

Ready position   *Roll upper body keeping arm in position*   *Fire the reverse punch*

Squared off with your opponent

Raising up the forearm to draw your opponent's attention

Firing the reverse punch into the opening

THE FRED KING SPECIAL

This is somewhat like the Tom Levak special except that when you move in, you do a rising block with the lead arm. The fast raise of the lead arm will approximate the initial action of the backfist enough that your opponent will react to it. He might raise his arm to defend. He might lean away. It doesn't matter as you can follow up with the reverse punch. I have a picture of Fred and myself in a match and both of us are in the rising block position with our rear hands cocked after the punch was thrown. When you don't know what had just happened, it is a hilarious picture. If you fight with your lead arm lowered, the speed of the action is enough to get your opponent's attention.

Ready Position

Rising block as you move in

Fire the reverse punch into the opening

THE ROBERT EDWARDS SPECIAL

Robert is a friend of mine who lives in Tacoma, Washington and is the smoothest heavyweight fighter I've ever seen. He's got this way of gliding at you rather than explosively taking off. It is deceptive. The way he does it he never looks like he's committing until he's on top of you.

What he does is set you up with a rhythmic bouncing, drawing his lead foot in on one bounce and extending it on the next, back and forth, back and forth. This is done with incredible relaxation. He'll do the same with his lead hand synchronized with his lead foot. What you don't catch is while he is doing this, he is creeping forward in very small increments until on the hand extension he touches his opponent's lead hand. Then he lunges in and hits with the reverse punch. He'll gauge whether he is going to go by whether he can touch his opponent's hand or not. By that time he has lulled his opponent to sleep by the bounce and is too close for them to react. It looks like he walks

THE CALIFORNIA BLITZ 1980s STYLE

I don't know who came up with this variation but I do know who made it famous. Steve "Nasty" Anderson, former 3 time #1 fighter was the prime exponent of this technique.

The key point of the delivery of this type of take off is based on a practical joke. Remember some time when you were standing with your weight on your back leg and someone came up and popped your knee, buckling it? That is what you do - on purpose. You buckle the lead knee to provide the suddenness of the take off. The trick here is to put yourself off balance forward so that your take off will be quick.

When you buckle the lead knee, make sure that your upper body and punch goes forward at the same time so that the entire action will be explosive. I can't stress this enough. Suddenness is the key to this. On the receiving end this is a very deceptive technique.

A good way of learning this is to do it coming down from a lead leg kick. Round kick is the easiest. When you land, instead of setting down firmly, let the knee buckle forward. It may take you awhile to get used to it but when you do, you'll find it useful. The upper body coming forward is a good way to get your weight into the punch.

Example of the old school trick of coming up behind someone and buckling their knee. The same is used in the Blitz.

The buckle of the lead knee is drastic and causes the body to lurch forward. Full sequence on next page.

The California Blitz done from a standing (or bouncing) position.

Buckling the lead knee when coming down from a kick will also set up a blitz (below).

BROKEN RHYTHM FROM JAPAN

When I fought on the 1983 USA AAU National Karate team against the visiting Japan national team, I expected to see some technically very sharp but immobile fighters. Was I ever in for a surprise! I saw some of the best broken rhythm I had ever seen and a lot of my teammates got suckered by it. The action is what I call a short step-long step. It was beautiful.

The idea is your first move gets you close enough to get a response but not close enough to get hit. Your second move is the explosive move that gets in too quickly to be countered. The technical action is this: You do a short, quick lunge at your opponent, almost close enough to be reached by him. Your guideline is that if he counter punches, he'll miss by an inch or two. If he does counter punch, *as his punch retracts,* you lunge in and hit. You can also lunge in if he checks his punch, seeing that you didn't fully commit. If he does nothing, then lunge in right away as you will be too close for him to react speedily.

The beauty of this technique is that you lunge in far enough to get him to feel as if you're really coming. He'll flinch, tighten up, begin to counter punch, whatever. He spots you aren't really coming in and begins to relax or cut short his move. At that moment you fully commit to your attack and catch him flat footed. This whole sequence takes about a second to execute.

Watch for two things: 1) You have to come in far enough on the short step. You'll blow the whole set up if you don't. 2) You have to make sure that you have a break in between your first and second step to get your opponent off guard. Timing is crucial here. If you want, go in expecting to block a counter punch on the way in. This technique has worked for me in all types of competition. You can do other follow up attacks besides the reverse punch.

Typical scene in the Pacific Northwest during the late 1970's, Fred King (L) and I battling it out. The only thing different in this photo is me throwing a reverse punch on him. He was the reverse punch specialist We fought 6 times and and each one was a barnstormer.

Illustration of the Short Step-Long Step.
You do a short burst at your opponent. This prompts him to counter punch your action.

You stop your move short of his ability to hit you. As he withdraws his punch, you draw your rear foot forward.

You explode forward and hit him with a reverse punch. The key to this move is to explode forward as he retracts his punch. Quite often he will relax slightly when doing so. Your explosion will take him off guard.

DEFENSIVE REVERSE PUNCH

I am going to show three different types of throwing the defensive reverse punch. The first is practical for fighting. The second one depends on how hard you can naturally hit for its effectiveness. The third one is great for tournaments and worthless for fighting.

The *first defensive reverse* punch keys off of your hip and shoulder action. Your opponent begins to come in and you crank your hip and shoulder *forward at him,* firing the punch. When you do this you get full hip and body rotation into the punch. This is a good move for an aggressive fighter. You meet your opponent's aggressive move with an aggressive move. Rotate and fire the punch at the same time. This way your punch will dig in deep.

The *second defensive reverse punch* is based on a flinch. It is utterly worthless as a fighting technique but quite a good one for competition. These days it is only necessary that you tag your opponent with a technique. Often it will not matter if you didn't have anything behind it or not. This counter punch takes advantage of the flinch by keying off of the lead shoulder. You *pull it backwards* as your opponent comes in. The pulling backward will create the mechanics of rotation and firing the rear hand. This is a surprisingly fast action. It hasn't any real power but you'll get enough range and speed out of it to get you a point.

The *third defensive reverse punch* I call "shake my hand." You use independent motion in throwing this punch. If you have good enough hand speed you can deliver quite a shock to the face of your opponent. Technically you just extend your hand from our position the same as you would if you were going to shake his hand. It just goes straight forward without any set up or body action. This is a speed punch which is not dependent on any other part of the body.

Beginning position (L)

Photo 1 - aggressive (r)

Photo 2 - flinch style (far right)

"Shake my hand"

Here are some examples of defensive reverse punch. They are illustrated top to bottom so that you can see the flow of action as well as the differences between the two. In the aggressive style, the puncher drives forward into his opponent with a hard punch. In the flinching style the puncher actually leans away from his attacker, pulling the attacker's target further away while slipping in the punch. This one is faster while the former is more effective. The "shake my hand" style is illustrated on the next page.

Aggressive style defensive reverse punch (below)   *Flinching style defensive reverse punch (below)*

1. Preparation   1. Preparation

2. Rear shoulder goes forward   2. Lead shoulder pulls back

3. Drive punch home   3. Extend punch

Defensive reverse punch continued. Shake my hand style. Your opponent starts to attack and you quickly fire the punch. This method is better if your opponent is a little inside of range and is not much of a kicker. Your hand extension will be faster than he can come in at you.

DEFENSIVE JUMP PUNCH

This is the technique I used to beat Keith Vitali, the number 1 rated fighter at the time at the 1979 Mid-America Diamond Nationals. I knew that when I put him into overtime, Keith liked to take the initiative and score his point fast. I had used this technique many times in the past in exactly the same circumstances. I always liked to bait my opponent into chasing me and then running into my technique. The same thing happened here. Keith came at me and I backed up, keeping the same distance between us. Then I jumped straight up. Since he was still coming in at me, he crossed the distance between us and ran into my punch. Point, and match. As you see in the photos the trick here is to keep the distance the same between you and your opponent as you back up. If your out run him, he'll stop chasing you.

This is not necessarily a weak move. This move has provided two knockouts that I have personally witnessed. Actually, one I delivered and the other I received so I can personally attest to the effectiveness of this move.

Your opponent starts forward. You draw back with your rear foot and down into a squat.

As your opponent closes the distance with his next step, you are jumping in the air to deliver the punch.

ANGLE REVERSE PUNCH

This is a technique Keith Vitali beat me with. As I mentioned in the section on Angling, you can off angle a straight line fighter. One of the things I knew about Keith was that when the chips were down, his bread and butter technique was the left hand backfist. We went into overtime down in San Jose at the West Coast Nationals in 1980. I was prepared. I set myself up to cover his left hand backfist and counter punch him in the ribs. We squared off. He came at me and...angled off to his left and reverse punched me! My punch missed him by a mile.

This is a good move to use to avoid getting hit if your opponent likes to fire as you move. You take the target right out of the line of his fire.

You roll over your lead knee off to your forward side angle and fire the reverse punch into your opponent's oncoming body.

THE LAUNCH (The "Blitz" for the new millennium)

This is a more recent discovery. I was going over some video taped matches with a Black Belt student of mine, Tim Gustavson, and I saw this interesting variation of a take off. The guy on the tape seemed to fire forward very suddenly and catch his opponent off guard and flat-footed. So I watched him intently and spotted an interesting variation of the blitz. Technically it goes like this.

You are in a wide stance. Draw your lead foot back 2/3 of the distance of the stance with the toes pointing forward. Here's the hard part. As you do this, *do not shift your weight back*. Drawing your lead foot back this far will put your body weight forward, way forward. Use lead foot's push to add to the weight coming forward and you'll take off like a rocket. Ensure that you fire your hit at the same time.

If you do this move correctly, there is no way you can do it slowly. The draw of your lead foot and keeping your shoulders fully forward will set you up to either launch or fall down. Use the bend of the lead knee to thrust yourself forward. This coupled with your weight forward will ensure a successful launch.

Illustrated here is a defensive use of the Launch as a defensive action. In this usage you use the pull back of the lead foot to evade your opponent's kick and launch for your counter attack. I left the first two photos "partner-less" so that you can see the foot and body positioning.

Right as your opponent begins his footwork, you draw your lead foot back...

...to the point where the side kick misses by a hair. Use the draw back to initiate the launch.

Using a launch back fist to smother my opponent's kick. This photo was taken at the 1974 Seattle Open Karate Championships. I was fighting Mark Kaliciak for the lightweight title.

"DINK – BOOMP!"

This is a particular favorite of mine. Where the preceding technique relies on an explosive initial move, this one is very soft. The "dink" is a soft forward jump of maybe 2-3 inches. In the photos, you see a high jump. This is just to emphasize the distance and the relaxation of the dink. The soft jump should be so subtle, low to the ground and short distanced that your opponent is not alerted by your action. As you land, you use that motion to explode in on him. For a follow up you can use a kick as well as a punch. Both are illustrated.

One of the hardest things to illustrate in a photo is the degree of relaxation you need for this action. I have over emphasized the height in the photos. Actually, you would not go higher than an inch or two. This way, the preparation for the take off is not compromised. You do the "dink" so relaxedly so as to disguise the fact that you are actually going to explode on your opponent. You need patience to do this.

The "dink-boomp" is also a good set up for a kick. You use the dink to get ever so slightly in range and then fire the front leg. In this example Tim uses a round kick. I found that the side kick worked better for me.

This was published in Black Belt magazine. I am scoring on Ritsu Goto in the lightweight finals at the 1970 Western States Karate Championships.

ANGLE BACKFIST

This is a good technique to use if you don't have the time to step out of your opponent's way. You tilt your body slightly to your lead side, rotate and backfist with your lead hand. This is a quick and economical motion. When you lean, make sure you get your head and torso out of the way of the attack. You can use a lead foot forward step or a rear leg turn if you have the time to do it. Strike as you lean. Don't lean and then strike. This is a good move against someone who commits on his attack but not against someone who fakes. Use it for someone who takes off fast.

PENDULUM BACKFIST (Snake Charmer)

A pendulum is a cord or rod with a weight attached to the bottom of it. When it is rocked, it will swing back and forth. If you have ever seen a hypnotist putting his victim to sleep by having him look at a watch swing back and forth, you have seen a pendulum. I also call this the snake charmer because of the lulling effect of the hand swaying back and forth. I learned this from watching a California fighter, Bob Halliburton.

You can use this motion to disguise the delivery of the backfist. You loosely swing your hand back and forth across the center line. In the photos note the relaxed position of the hand. On one of the swings, you release the backfist towards your opponent's head. The idea here is to let it flow off from the swinging motion so that there is no telegraph to it. Make sure that you don't bring it back or cock it first. That will be enough of a break in the flow to alert your opponent to it.

Example of the Pendulum Back Fist on an opponent
The key here is that when you move the hand back and forth, you do this within the natural movement of your hand. Don't stand immobile and then start to move it. You'll alert your opponent that you're up to something.

LOW ROUND KICK

This is the technique I was known around the country for. I've hit darn near everybody I've fought with it. There are some who've escaped but not many. The thing about this kick is practically everybody knew it was coming. Many knew it was going to be a round kick. Few ever stopped it. It won many a match for me and I developed it so that I could throw it off of either leg.

Many areas in the U.S. no longer allow the groin as a target area for tournaments. I feel this is a major mistake. Many schools use what is allowed in tournaments to set the parameters of how their sparring is developed. While tournament expansion was the reason for the great technical and strategic boom of karate sparring between 1967-1980, this is the same reason for the decline in effectiveness of the techniques since then.

Up through 1980 almost all techniques and targets were allowed and so offenses and defenses had to be researched and refined all through that era. You take away certain targets in competition and you don't have to train to defend against them. You do this across all of the belt divisions over a period of time and you'll have a watered down method of fighting which is less and less real as time goes on. As it is, the low round kick has almost fallen into disuse.

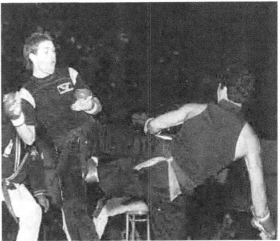

Against Flem Evans (above L), Phil Lovings (below L), Bobby Wilson (above R) and Bill Rooklidge (below R)

There are two points which make this kick quicker than the usual round kick. First is the bend of the kicking leg. You use only the bend you have in your stance. Don't pick it up and bend it. That'll just slow it down. Just use the bend you have.

The second point is that the kick doesn't have to come from the side as in the usual round kick. It comes straight from the floor to the target. Since the groin is easy to hurt, the groin kick doesn't have to have as much power as a kick to anywhere else on the body. This same kick to the body is useful as a distraction or to get you a point but will hurt nothing. The sharpness in this kick is more than enough to drop someone.

I do this kick with either a lunge or a skip footwork. The lunge is used in the photos. Keep in mind the kick and footwork are done *suddenly*. Don't drift into it. Explode!

Notice the extension in the full speed delivery of this kick.
Against Earl Squalls circa 1976

SPIN KICK COUNTER TO A ROUND KICK

This is a very simple move to do and you can use this to counter the preceding technique. The key is in the timing of the counter. Begin your spinning action as your opponent comes in for his round kick. This way as his kick nears completion your counter will be under way or fully fired. The importance of the spin as he begins is that the spin will shift his intended target. I show the spin side kick in the photos but the hook kick is equally effective.

Below is where I used this technique to deliver a spin hook kick as a counter Instead of firing to the head, I shot it low and got the point. My opponent is Bob Smith from Canada. The photo is from circa 1978.

STEP AWAY SIDE KICK

This is a technique that both Keith Vitali and Mike Genova excelled in. Right when you thought you had them where you could run right over the top of them, they backed up far enough away to get that kick in. Sometimes the kick was called as a push but the opponent got the message, "Chase me and you'll get kicked."

Where others failed in trying to duplicate this kick was in the initial move. You don't pick up the kick leg and then kick. Often the kick could get jammed if the opponent was fast. The secret to this kick is that you step away *with your rear leg first*. Then you use the tight chambering of the lead leg to add to the distance between you and your opponent. That way you *do* gain a little distance first. Try it first just pulling the lead leg up and then try it with the step away and see for yourself. The step away method will give you the range for the kick.

You can do the same with a *jump away* side kick. This is done with a leap using the pull of the kick leg to create altitude. When you step away you can plant and hit like a hammer. This is the way both Ray McCallum and Fred King used it. When you jump away it is more of a point karate move. I have used either way, myself.

HAIR LINE DEFENSE

A miss is as good as a mile. "Hairlining" is my term for making your opponent miss by just a hair. This is a skill I had that frustrated many an opponent. It would seem that I was just in reach. Then, as he barely missed me, bang. I'd hit him back. Two of the methods I used are shown here. Once you get the idea you can create more.

The first is an *extension step* and you use this when your stance is fairly shallow. It consists of taking a step back with your rear foot far enough away for your opponent's attack to fall short. Notice in the photos that I am ready to return fire. This is important.

The second is a *contracting step*. Here you're in a somewhat larger stance and you pull your lead foot back, again far enough to make your opponent miss. This one is good for a counter kick set up.

What is crucial is that you need to extend or contract enough for him to miss his first shot *and* leave you in a position to counter. You want to back up just enough to catch him *in between* attacks. Once you get the hang of it, it is a deceptively simple, yet, effective defense.

Example of an extension step and counter punch against a side kick

Example of a contraction step against a round kick

Example of an execution of a contracting step and counter hook kick against Mark Kaliciak. He was one of my main rivals in the lightweight division in the Pacific Northwest.

UNDER KICKS

This is another technique I was known for, the defensive groin kick. What better way is there to keep a high kicker honest? There are many areas of the country who do not allow groin kicks so, in those areas, I dealt with high kick differently. But in the areas where they were legal, I used these techniques to keep those legs down.

The Lift Kick - I was introduced to this by Tip Hanzlik, a classmate of mine. He was actually better at this technique than anyone I met on the competition circuit. I loved to kick high and one night he made me pay for it. The move is incredibly simple and speedy. You just shift your weight to the back leg and lift the front. This is good against any type of lateral (round, side, hook) kick. The key is to just shift back, not step back.

Back Kick - This is a rather easy way to counter a rear leg front kick or round kick. You do this when you are "cross stance," your left leg forward to his right. Right as your opponent starts to kick, you pivot away on the balls of your feet and aim the kick along his extended leg. Aiming the kick along the extended leg is a sure way to actually hit the groin.

Example of an under back kick against a flying kick. This photo was taken in Texas. The opponent is Norris Williams.

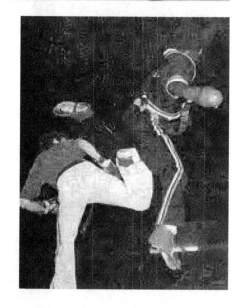

Round Kick - This is used against a lead leg side kick or round kick. With your opponent facing you "same side," left leg to left leg forward, you just lean away from his kick and pop up a round kick that lays across his groin.

Bill Rooklidge, my first black belt, executing an under round kick to me in a tournament. I encouraged my Black Belts to compete and do their best rather than bow out.

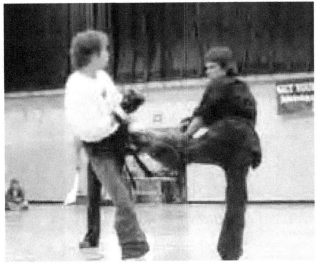

Side Kick - I often use this when my opponent is facing me cross stance. He begins to kick with a side kick or round kick, lean away and fire. Note: In all of these remember to keep your guard up to protect yourself against his kick. If you miss the counter kick you'll be glad you did.

Side under kick against Steve Fisher at the 1980 Battle Of Atlanta. Steve was, himself, a master of the low round kick and under kick.

THE MANIAC ROUND KICK - PUNCH

This is a favorite of mine and could actually be included in the sucker move category. How many times have you fought a white belt and had to fight for your life because he was throwing wild, swing for the fence kicks? That is what this move is based on. You crank up what looks like the wildest, swing round kick and when your opponent reacts (and most will) you hit him with a punch to the face. This is almost too simple. What makes it work is the absolute lack of any semblance of control of the kick. Throw it wild enough and you *will* get a reaction. Make sure that you fire the punch immediately as he reacts and not set your foot down first.

THE CHICAGO RIDGE HAND

This is based on your opponent flinching. The take off is basically the same as the California blitz, using the front knee buckle. When you take off, your opponent's flinch is increased by the wide swing of your ridge hand. It looks like you're swinging for the fence. Timing of your take off is a critical point. Picking the right opponent is just as critical. Freddie Letuli of Chicago was a prime exponent of this, as well as "Scorpion" Burrage. I've seen Freddie blow away opponents with this. I also saw John Longstreet break his nose by hitting him when he came in on him. He was ready for it. Like I said, the pick of who you do this to is critical.

Two things you can do to increase the workability of this technique are to fully commit yourself on the take off and angle your upper body slightly off to one side. This will get your nose out of the way.

A key point is to angle your head off to the side so that you don't get hit with a counter punch.

LEAD JAB - ROUND KICK

This rather simple technique is ideal to use against a leaner, the guy who fades away from the high punch. I used this when I fought one of the Japanese national team members back in 1983. He would lean away from a lead jab and come immediately back with a reverse punch. To counter this I attacked with a lead jab to his face. He leaned away as I predicted...right into the range for my round kick. Whack! That surprised him. He moved away rather than leaning after that. You can also use a double kick with this. Jab and fire the kick, hesitate and fire the kick again when he starts to come out of his lean.

Catching Jim MacDonald of Canada with this technique. This photo came from my coming out of retirement tournament in 1977 This was the Grand Championship match and it was against a tough "Jimmy Mac."

LEG TAP - BACKFIST

This technique is the one which set me up to fight for the lightweight championship match in the 1972 International Karate Championships. This was the first major tournament I reached the finals in and was the springboard for my national career. I've used this technique for 30 years and it still works. The trick of this technique is that you tap the leg rather than sweep it. The tap is for distraction purposes only. As the leg taps, fire the backfist. Important note: you use the amount of leg bend in the stance and pop it from the floor. You don't need to pick it up and slam it into your opponent's leg. That'll just slow it down and might set you up for falling yourself if he picks up his leg.

Here I'm going after Chip Wright of Medford, Oregon with the leg tap. Chip is one of the finest technicians I have ever had the pleasure to know or fight.

GUARD POSITIONS

There are several different types of covers I teach in my school which are good in point fighting. These guard positions work because of the covering that the hand pads provide and the fact you can't get a point called against you if an attack hits a padded area.

The first I call *the Wrap*. Your lead hand covers the side of your head and the rear hand covers your ribs. As your opponent attacks, you cover against his first attack and on contact, fire your counter (see photos).

Here's an example of the Wrap defense against a back fist. The idea is that when your opponent moves, you immediately wrap and take the shot on the glove. On touch contact you return fire. In the Pacific Northwest, the prime exponents of this defense were Robert Edwards, Mel Cherry and Steve Curran. Robert had such exceptional timing that he would wait until the last moment to cover. This was very frustrating as you felt you had the shot in and then, bang, it was taken away.

Example of a reverse punch thrown in this style. Often, a reverse punch thrown under an opponent's guard was very effective. I was shown this by Bob Barrow, a student of Chuck Norris. His group was well known for this style of reverse punch.

The second I call *the Shell*. You cover your ribs and groin with your lead arm and your head with your rear hand. This is a widely used position in tournaments today. From this position you can sneak punch. I've done it a number of times and it never fails to throw an opponent off.

Example of the Shell against a reverse punch

Keith Vitali (L), the #1 rated karate player for the majority of tournament career, was a master of the Shell defense.

The third came from necessity. I call it *the Fender*. The shot I got hit with the most was the backfist. This came to me while I was training for an A-rated tournament. I figured out that I could put my arm in a position which would present an obstruction to both the backfist and the following reverse punch without looking like I was doing so. Take a look at the photos as it is hard to describe accurately. Put your lead hand face high and keep the elbow in front of your ribs. Look in a mirror and compare with the photos how you look and see if you have the same position. From this position you can sneak punch or sneak backfist rather easily.

The Fender is a good position to deliver sneak punches. As you can tell from the photos, you don't have to do any kind of preliminary positioning or repositioning in or der to deliver the reverse punch or the lead jab. You can use these either offensively or as an immediate counter offense. The defensive approaches Hit as the Ranges Cross and hold Your Position and Hit are especially useful for this position.

This technique closes out this chapter. Simple moves are the first ones I will teach a student when he learns how to spar. The simple moves are the basics upon which the following chapters; Complex Moves and Sucker Moves are based. All of the simple moves have a couple common basics: timing, distancing and positioning. If you are in position you can move without any other set up. If your timing is right you will hit your opponent when he isn't ready. If your distancing is good you will not get hit without his telegraphing it first. Put these three factors in with any simple move and the chances of it hitting will greatly increase.

COMPLEX MOVES

A complex move is governed by having one of two aspects: 1) it is physically difficult to do or 2) your opponent has to be in the right position for you to pull it off. In fighting, complex moves are risky. In tournament fighting they are less so. They are crowd pleasers and nothing will get a judge to call a point faster than the successful execution of a complex move. In the previous section on Simple Moves, I did not mean to imply that a champion only does simple moves. In *any* champion's bag of tricks are several wild card moves to pull out when the time is right. Many times complex moves are just that, wild card maneuvers, the unexpected tactic. While these are not the every time approach, they'll often be enough of a shift to catch the other guy off guard for you to score a point and win the match.

The complex moves which are physically difficult to execute are also ones which need your opponent to be set up for them. Jump kicks, drop kicks, takedowns and so forth all fall in this category. Then there are certain complex moves which require your opponent respond in a certain way. Either way you look at it, these are a step above the execution of a simple move.

It is easier to work a complex move on a less experienced fighter. He is more apt to react in a certain way every time, for example, leaning away from a head high kick. His inexperience will allow him to be set up without the set up being recognized. Simple moves are better against an experienced fighter but it is good to have a few wild card maneuvers handy as they can be suckered, too. Here are some examples of complex moves.

Executing a full leg sweep on Ferdie Orbino at the 1974 Seattle Open Karate Championships

THE OLLIE JONES SPECIAL

Back when I was an under belt, we had this guy in our school named Ollie Jones. He was about 6'4" and had this one takedown and he'd nail everyone in our school with this. I stole it from him and used it to good effect in tournaments. Basically it is a cross behind step, grab and front leg cut. The peculiar thing about this throw is that it cuts in front of the legs than the standard cut from behind. When you cut in front of your opponent's legs, his first reaction is to put both hands forward the floor to protect his face from hitting the floor. This saves you from having to save him during the fall and allows you to follow up hit right away.

Ollie liked to use this against stationary opponents. I, however, found that I worked it best against a jumping opponent. Against a jumper you have to take a lead step first to cover the distance when you move in. (Note: the action of cutting in front of the legs and behind the rear of the legs is the same so I include them both of them under the name of the OJ Special.)

Illustrated here is the application of the OJ Special against an opponent who leaps in the air for the counter attack. Take care in training to not just carelessly dump your opponent on his head. This photo is from circa 1973 at the Northwest Invitational Karate Championships.

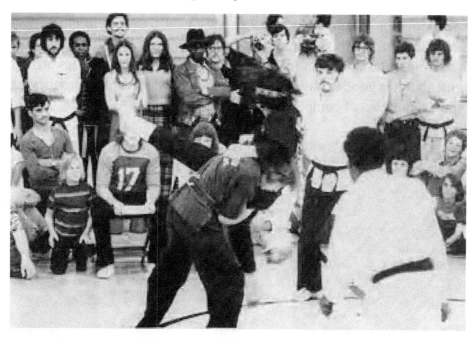

The Ollie Jones Special. Throw your back fist past the checking hand as a distraction.

Grab your opponent's shoulder as you cross behind step to set up the throw.

Cut in front of your opponent's shin and pull forward at the same time. Follow up with the punch.

  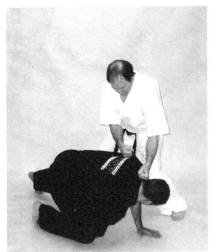

THE JANITOR SWEEP

Robert Edwards, who has another technique quoted earlier, had this nickname. He was "The Janitor." He swept everything (everyone) in his path. I once saw him sweep an opponent three times in a row in a championship match. Scored each time. Three up, three down, just like that. He sets up the sweep with a drifting backfist, taking a long lead step. Then he does a cross over step with his rear leg. With his extended arm he crosses his opponent's body and cuts him out with a sweep behind the legs. Look a the photos as you read this to get a good picture of it. The main trick to this is to cut out his legs while he is still moving. This way his feet aren't planted and are easy to cut out.

THE MAINENTI SWEEP

The Mainenti sweep is basically the same sweep coming off of a reverse punch rather than a backfist. I was introduced to this sweep the hard way. I fought Rich Mainenti for the Seattle Open Karate Championships back in 1972. He literally flipped me head over heels with this sweep. The fact that I liked to jump up and backfist didn't help me one bit and it sure aided him. I found out from a student of his years later just how he did this.

What you do is this. You do an extended lead step and reverse punch, chest high, *past your opponent*. This is a calculated miss and puts your arm across his body. You cut behind his rear legs while applying counter pressure against the chest. The legs will go and he will be on the ground. What is essential in this technique is the commitment of the first step as it will get you in close enough to cut both legs.

Note that you cut all the way through with your sweep leg when you do the sweep. Then, don't forget to check your opponent's leg as you go down to punch him.

ROUND KICK INTO SIDE KICK

The next couple of techniques show how one kick can introduce an opening for a follow up kick to land. The first is where you throw a round kick to get your opponent to cover as a defense. As he covers you pull it back into a side kick chamber position. This is important. You do not want to recoil the round kick as you usually do and then chamber into a side kick position. This takes too much time. Pull back the round kick as if you had thrown a side kick (as if you were wiping your foot off on his jacket) so that you can pump the follow up side kick immediately into the opening. This type of recoil takes a bit of practice but once you get it, it will flow.

A key to doing this kick swiftly is when you do your step up and chamber for the round kick, pivot your standing leg however much you need to fire the side kick. This way when you pull back from the round kick, you will not need to mover your body at all, only your kick leg.

SIDE KICK INTO ROUND KICK

This is basically the reverse of the preceding technique. You shoot the side kick to your opponent's middle, recoil it as if you'd just thrown a round kick and then fire the round kick to the head. As the round kick is a snapping kick thrown off the knee, this is a much faster kick.

This kick has been a particular favorite of mine. I worked on it so that I could throw it equally well with either leg.

HOOK KICK INTO ROUND KICK

Bill Wallace was the master at this one. He would use this against a leaner, someone who would lean away from his hook kick to the head. As his opponent would come back in to throw his counter punch, he'd find the round kick meeting him. The awesome thing about Wallace is that he had such phenomenal balance that it didn't matter if his opponent hesitated before he came in or not. Bill would just stand there with his leg chambered and pop him when he did come in.

JUMP AWAY SPINNING SIDE KICK

The first time I saw this technique I was at the 1980 Mid-America Diamond Nationals watching the match between "Scorpion" Burrage and John Longstreet. Right at a moment when "Scorpion" was charging, John leapt *away,* spun and nailed him with a solid kick...which wasn't called for a point. I stood there with my mouth hanging open. I had used many times a jump spin side kick but I had never seen anyone jump *away* and hit somebody with it. I went home and worked on it. Several years later I was fighting #1 rated fighter, Steve "Nasty" Anderson up in Tacoma, Washington and that was the first point I scored on him. This one did get called for me.

OFFENSIVE SIDE DROP KICK

The defensive side drop kick has been around since the competitive days of Mike Stone, 1963 or so. The twist on this is that I use it offensively. This is good to use on an opponent who likes to guard against your moving in by raising his knee. If you have ever played baseball and slid into home plate, you have the idea. You step in and drop straight to the floor. Bracing your arms on the floor, you use the momentum of the drop and push your body to slide forward. This is usually enough to cover the remaining distance to your opponent. As you come under his leg, shoot your kick straight up. I pulled this on Roy Kurban at the US Championships in 1973.

You need to be certain that your opponent will raise his leg as you come in or you will be left in a most compromising position. When you get an opponent who will accommodate you, this is a great shot to get in.

JAMMED PUNCH - LEG SWEEP

A lot of defensive action is done by guarding your body rather than blocking. This means your set up actions need to take this into account. A favorite of mine is when my opponent likes to cover against a body punch.

What I do is this: I come in and reverse punch to the body. He covers. Instead of retracting my punch I add my other arm and give him a slight shove upwards. When he goes off balance I cut with my rear leg behind his leg for the sweep (or legs for the take down) and then follow up with a punch.

Foot sweeping Ferdie Orbino at the Seattle Open Karate Championships

SPIN HOOK INTO AX KICK

As the back of the head is no longer a valid target in tournament karate, this is a move not much used anymore but it is a goodie. When your opponent has a habit of ducking hook kicks you can shift your hips and drop the leg on him like an ax. This should cure this ducking business. A safety note: you need a good deal of thigh strength to control this kick and the weight of your leg increases the momentum of the dropping kick.

HOOK KICK - FOOT HOOK

This is a good move against an opponent who likes to lean away in a deep stance. Set him up with a few high kicks to establish that this is what he likes to do. Then shoot the hook kick and when he leans away, follow it through to come around behind his lead leg and cut the leg out from under him. Don't just bang the leg. Hook it at the ankle and yank it. This move is done in a flowing motion.

The trick on this action is to catch his ankle while he is still leaning back.

TAKE DOWN COUNTERS AGAINST KICKS

This is another series of techniques that have fallen into disuse because of them no longer being allowed in tournament competition. With the emphasis on fancy kicking being the spectator draw, defenses against kick such as under kicks or takedowns are disallowed. Too bad because these actions are effective and will make a kicker more judicious in his choice of targets.

Against a round kick – Your partner kicks at you and you cross block the kick. This type of block allows you to use the down arm to catch the kick. You step in, grab your opponent and cut his base leg out from under him. Notice that in the photos I am very close to him so that I can control his body on the way down to the floor. In a self defense situation you'd just let him drop. Follow up with a punch to your downed opponent.

Against a side kick – As your opponent comes in with his side kick, you angle step to his rear letting his kick go past you. Slide your rear arm under his leg and catch it. Follow up step and grab him, using your other leg to cut out his base leg. Follow up with a punch.

Against a spin hook kick – In this one you step in at a slight angle (so as not to catch a spin side kick in the ribs when you thought it was a hook kick) and execute a cross block catch. Note in the photos I am catching him at the thigh. Grab him and hook your foot *in front* of his leg. This takedown puts him face forward toward the floor. As he keeps his head from hitting the floor, you maneuver him for the counter punch.

The photo below came from a match with Jimmy Tabares. I mention him later in the best matches I have ever seen section.

Oklahoma City, 1980

Rear hoist against a spin kick – This one has a funny story. I was back east, Atlanta, Georgia, I think. I had demonstrated this move to the current #1 fighter in the country, Keith Vitali. He called over a student of his, Vernon Johnson. Vernon was an up and coming fighter and was a heavyweight. I was around 155 pounds at the time. He told Vernon that I could pick him up and throw him down. Vernon, keeping his manners in, said nothing but the look said it all. "This little guy is not picking me up." So, I had him do a kick. Hoist and dump. The resultant look on his face said it all. "Whoa!"

The secret of this move is to get your hips under your opponent's so that when you pop your hips forward, you lift with your legs. Once he is off the ground a quick twist of your arms will aim him towards the floor where you can punch him.

SUCKER MOVES

This section deals with throwing your opponent a curve ball. The idea is that if the fast ball doesn't get him, throw the curve ball. I divide these "curve balls" into three categories: variable basics, change up techniques and Twilight Zone moves. Variable basics are slight shifts in the standard basic techniques. These are techniques with an odd angle to them. Change up techniques are those which start out being one technique and shift into something else mid move. Twilight Zone moves are named right after the old TV series, "The Twilight Zone," where the odd and unexpected happened.

There is a common element in each of these three. Your opponent will have been suckered, but good. Collectively these are called Sucker moves. Sucker moves are thoroughly demoralizing. Anyone can truly appreciate being caught with a good move. Nobody likes being made a chump. Once you get how these are done and practice them a bit, you'll appreciate them.

An example of the Bill Wallace hook kick on James Faison in Seattle, 1974.

CANNONBALL ROUND KICK

An old student of mine called this the Grandfather kick. You set your opponent up with a cannonball back kick, which is a back kick thrown from a tuck position. It resembles what is called a cannonball dive into a pool of water. The kick is a back kick that travels parallel to the floor. You set your opponent by banging him with this kick. On the next one, instead of firing the kick from the tuck position, continue raising your foot so that it is positioned over your hip and knee pointing at him. From there fire a downward round kick to his neck. The first time you pull this one off you should see his eyes widen a bit. He expects an impact on his arm and all of a sudden sees a kick coming at his head.

This is how your set up your opponent for this kick. First you fire off a back kick.
(continued next page)

Using the same body positioning as the back kick, raise the foot up higher than the hip and then fire downward.

Firing a cannonball kick at Chip Wright. Sometimes you connect, sometimes you don't.

BILL WALLACE ROUND KICK

Bill "Superfoot" Wallace has been acknowledged as the greatest kicker of American tournament karate history. His accuracy, timing and balance is legendary. I worked with him a couple of times and learned a lot from him. His round kick is his trademark. He chambers his round kick as if he is throwing a side kick. The edge of his foot faces you. He then rolls his ankle to face the instep towards you and fires the kick. It is very deceptive and quick.

(above photo) A split second before firing the Wallace round kick at Blair Orr from Canada

KEITH VITALI ROUND KICK

Keith does a very effective variation of the Wallace round kick. Keith chambers his side kick with his knee in towards his chest and foot on a line with his opponent. This is basically the same way I chamber my side kick and is a good set up for a power side kick. You pump your opponent with a couple of good, banging side kicks. From the chamber position, move the thigh in the hip socket over into the round kick position and then fire the round kick. This will not only give the impression a side kick is coming but the transferal of chamber positions will break rhythm for your opponent as well.

Ensure that you aim the edge of the foot at your opponent so that he registers your action as a side kick. That way he'll see the round kick too late, if at all.

BILL WALLACE HOOK KICK

Bill Wallace throws his round, side and hook kicks from the same chamber position. He sets up his opponent by hitting at him with a side kick and when his opponent gets used to the side kick coming from the high knee set up, Bill turns it into a hook kick to the head. This takes his opponent by surprise.

A good exercise for this is to brace yourself against the wall and put your knee up shoulder high with the foot facing your target. Extend your leg forward but at an angle in a side kick fashion. At full extension bend the knee and hook backwards with the heel. To practice the round kick from this position, rotate your foot and ankle from heel facing to instep facing and back again. This will set you up for the flip of the kick.

This photo was taken in San Jose and is one of my favorite magazine photos. My opponent was Sam Montgomery.

THE BREWER BOZO SHOT

This is a true sucker shot. I call it the Brewer Bozo shot because you feel like a bozo when you get hit with it. Eric Brewer came up with this. He's a student of Fred King and when I saw him do this I couldn't believe anybody was falling for this. Later, we sparred and I got hit with it. Twice. Then I reversed it on him and he got hit with his own move. Reading the description of it and looking at the photos will not do it justice. You have to do it on someone to truly appreciate it.

You throw a rear leg angle kick, lifting it and not snapping it, at your opponent's middle *without turning your body.* As he reacts, shoot the lead backfist to the head. The really funny part of this is that you don't have to throw the kick very hard to get your opponent's attention. Just pop the leg towards the fact and he'll look at it. (note: In Eric's defense he later went on to be the #1 rated heavyweight fighter in the North American Sport Karate Association.)

Of all the moves I have hit somebody with or have been hit with, this is the most stupid move I have ever seen. And I say that with admiration. Many sucker moves are slickly calculated to make someone zig when they should zag but this one is plainly stupid. It's wonderful.

CHICAGO RIDGE HAND - PUNCH

This one will make your opponent crawl up inside himself after he is hit with it. This is a great sucker move. You take off with the Chicago ridge hand (described earlier in the book) and as he reacts, you curve the hitting arm and punch the exposed ribs. If he covers rather than block, he'll flinch enough for you to pick a different target. This is usually good for one hit per opponent as they get wise awfully fast on this one.

A key to this move is to fold your arm at the elbow but not bring your whole arm down. This way the punch just slides from the ridge hand in one easy movement.

BACKFIST PASS - RIDGE HAND

At the 1981 Portland Pro-Am, Larry Kelly, who is usually a kicker, hit John Longstreet with this for a point. I don't think that he even meant this to be a sucker technique. He was chasing a backpedaling Longstreet and threw a backfist which missed. Instead of retracting the arm, he took a half step forward and turned it into a ridge hand which didn't miss.

I thought, "What if you threw the backfist *intentionally to miss?* Instead of throwing it at him, why not throw it just past him?" I went back to the school and began to work on it and found another sucker move to add to my bag of tricks. The principle is this: *Nobody ever throws a technique to intentionally miss.* All techniques, even if they are fakes, are thrown on target. Fascinating premise. So, if nobody ever throws a technique to miss, everybody expects the technique to come at them and will so defend against it. So, if you throw it to miss, they'll defend against it anyway. What a funny proposition, but it works.

You lunge in and throw the backfist on a trajectory to go past the face. Your opponent will automatically assume that it is a real attack and defend. The backfist never lands on the block (or cover). Right after it passes you pull it back as a ridge hand. The beauty of this move is that your opponent never realizes he's been had. This makes the technique workable over and over again.

THE McCALLUM DUCK & DUMP

Ray McCallum has never been accused of being the most orthodox of fighters. I witnessed this particular move at the 1979 Mid-America Diamond Nationals. His opponent, Peter Paik, fired a lunging side kick at him and then promptly lost him. Where'd Ray go? Underneath the side kick and came up on his back side where Peter couldn't see him. He then took him down and punched him. The crowd went crazy. This technique is great against the fighter who lunges heavily into his kick.

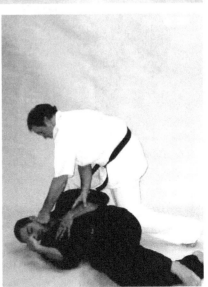

CHIP WRIGHT GROIN PUNCH

Chip Wright is a friend of mine and probably one of the most talented fighters I have ever fought or seen, bar none. His work ethic took this talent to great heights. He could do it all, kick, punch, you name it he could do it with either side. For all his talent, though, he had this one goofy move he'd use. A groin punch. The first time I saw Chip do this technique I thought, "I hope he never tries this one on me because if he does, he'll be in for a surprise." Well, he tried it and I think he was surprised at how easy I was to be hit with it.

This technique has less to do with guts than it does just knowing that your opponent is going to kick. When I first tried it I found that if you angle your body off to your front side a bit as you throw the punch, you get yourself out of the way of the kick coming at you. This technique is a great demoralizer. There's nothing that makes you feel quite as stupid as getting punched in the groin when you're trying to kick someone.

CROSS UNDER KICK

Out of every technique I have hit anyone with, this is my absolute favorite. The cross kick has gotten points for me and on one occasion, a disqualification. The nice thing about this kick is it is a flip that comes up directly under the groin so that it doesn't have to have much power to make quite an impact. Coming at the groin from underneath makes the protective cup rather useless so it is also a good "enforcer" for when things get a little out of hand. The trick for getting distance with this kick is to move the thigh and not just flip from the knee. You do this and you don't have to be quite so close to hit.

Interesting side note here. Watch your control with this kick. I got disqualified by hitting too hard with this one at the 1979 M.A.R.S. (Martial Arts Ratings System) National Karate Championships, preventing me from winning it for the second time.

SNEAK PUNCH FROM THE CLINCH

I found this one useful back in early 1980. What was happening was that a lot of fighters would lunge in with a back fist or reverse punch and then tie up their opponent. Then the action would stop for a few seconds before the chief referee called for a break. This was a sort of unwritten agreement of stopping if the technique didn't get in. Earlier in the season I had scored quite a bit with knees to the groin and there became a bit of an uproar about this. Knees after that weren't even allowed as attacking weapons and eventually the groin got taken away as a target.

I was fighting Sam Montgomery in Oakland and I found myself in the same position of having to clinch to keep him from scoring on me. Sam was powerful hitter and I didn't want to get hit so therefore, I tied his arms up whenever I could. In one exchange, I tied up his arms and pulled his head in towards me. He reacted by pulling his head back. I let his head go only so far back and while retaining my hold on his neck, I popped him in the face with my other hand and then pulled him back in to the clinch. I got the point.

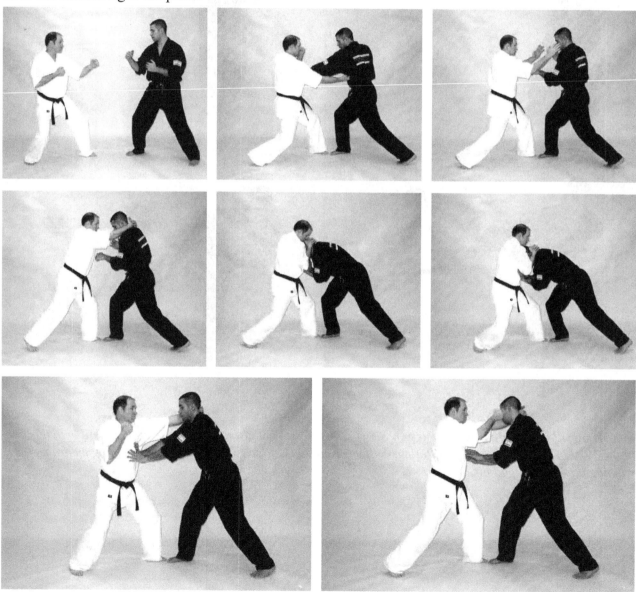

FACE KICK FROM BEHIND

Have you ever had an opponent throw a technique at you and then turn their back on you and cover up? Frustrating, isn't it? I used to do it all the time. I found a good counter for it. When a person turns their back and covers they usually cover the sides of their head because most tournaments don't permit the back of the neck to be struck, as it is a part of the spinal column. When they do this, their face is open. If you step towards their back at a slight angle and fire an angle kick right on a line with their armpit area, you'll the foot hitting in their face. The main thing is to step in deeply so that your leg will come up on the other side of their body. I nailed John Longstreet with this so hard that I almost knocked him out.

HOOKING SIDE KICK

In my school, the official name for this kick is the "incorrect side kick." It is the way every beginner throws a side kick before they can do it right. A correct side thrust kick comes straight from the chamber position, in a good, straight line. Well, when you get an opponent who protects their ribs with their elbow you have to abandon the straightness of the kick for a different angle.

For this kick, you chamber it like a round kick and circle it toward your opponent's ribs and just at the last few inches of extension, you rotate your hips into the kick and drive the heel forward. What happens is that you circle around the elbow then drive it straight in. This is good for when your opponent keeps a slightly sloppy guard and their elbow is off their ribs a bit.

On the next page is an example of a successful combination you can throw off of this kick.

A variation of this is what John Longstreet and Keith Vitali used to do. They'd bang their opponent on the arm with the incorrect side kick (or roundhouse heel kick if you want to think of it that way) and then pop the second kick to the head as a regular round kick. The first kick gets the opponent thinking "side kick" and when the round kick hits them, it comes as a surprise. Both kicks thrown in this fashion are very fast and I have worked them to good use myself.

Below is a shot of me firing this kind of kick at "Chicken" Gabriel. This was in San Diego circa 1980. "Chicken" was a very cagey fighter so I needed something equally as cagey to score and win the match.

SUICIDE STANCE

The next series is for the courageous and footworking fools. "Suicide Stance" is just a squared up position, which allows for maximum side to side movement. Your skill in range adjustment is crucial here. It is maddening to the opponent for you to face them with apparently all your targets exposed and they can't hit them. What you are doing is constantly making them readjust their position in relationship to you. You bounce on the periphery (outside edge of their range line in a circular fashion. You bounce back and forth, sometimes several steps to one side and then to the other and back again. With constant movement and a good eye for range and the connection line, this will actually become quite simple rather than dangerous for you. One note: for the sake of the photos, I am flat footed. Don't be flat footed when doing these techniques. Move on the balls of your feet.

The *first technique* is the easiest to work and is worked by a lot of fighters from the positions they normally use. This is the side step and jab. Here you are bouncing back and forth in front of your opponent and when they move, whichever direction you are going towards at that time, angle your body jab with that hand in that direction and jab with that hand.

What isn't shown here in the left photo is that you should be constantly moving side to side on the balls of your feet in this position. When you are already moving, it is easier to accelerate that movement in a defensive step.

The *second technique* is an offensive one and this is where you catch your opponent in mid shift from one position to another. What this is based on is this: your opponent will face you in whatever position they think or feel is the best for them. When you move off to the side, they will readjust themselves to get back into that position. If you are constantly moving, they are going to be constantly readjusting. This is where you get them. You go to the right, they go to their left to reposition. As they finish, you go back to your left. They now have to readjust. Right as they begin to readjust again, you attack. You catch them in mid action.

The *third technique* is a variation of the second one. Here you are facing your opponent. You start to take a step to your left and then you pull your foot back to its original position. Then you step to your right. Then you shift back and forth from your right to left to right to left quickly. This will resemble a basketball player trying to fake out their guard. This quick back and forth movement will befuddle your opponent just enough so that you will be able to catch them in transition from one position to another.

One of the safety factors of doing the Suicide Stance is that you are constantly moving so that any attack they might throw at you will at least be partially handled by your movement. This is also a good demoralizer as very few fighters do it so it is an unorthodox action and is unexpected. And it is fun to pull on someone.

CONCEPTUAL AIDS
AND ADDED INFORMATION

As in my first book, this is my favorite section. It contains essays, observations, evaluations, and personal notes, which I have collected and distributed to my students over the years. All of these pertain to the attainment of greater skill and understanding. They may not all have to deal directly with tournament fighting though. They represent ideas that have been going through my mind for years and refinements of other ideas I have previously published.

Ideas and their actualization are what breathe life into any art, whether it is martial or not. Some of these concepts may click with you and some may not. I have personally used each one of them at one time or another. One of the great challenges of my instructing has been how well can I communicate what I know so that the student will duplicate it. Since all people do not come out of one mold, there is no one teaching method that will ensure every student will get it. The constant search for different ways to teach the same thing to different people is the birth of this section and the same section in my previous book. Incidentally, I love the challenge. So, feel free to take any of these ideas and make them your own. This is what they are here for.

OFFENSIVE AND DEFENSIVE APPROACH COUNTERS

Most of the first book I wrote covers the offensive and defensive approaches quite thoroughly however I'm going to put them out here again for this book in a brief description.

OFFENSIVE APPROACHES:

DIRECT ATTACK: An attack that comes straight from you to your opponent without any set up. This is a singular attack.

Example of Direct Attack - Lunge back fist

ATTACK BY COMBINATION: This is a connected series of direct attacks, each one intending to score.

Example of Attack By Combination - back fist followed by reverse punch

INDIRECT ATTACK: Here is where you use a distraction of some kind (fake, broken rhythm, sweep, yell, etc.) to set your opponent for a follow up attack.

Example of Indirect Attack - Hip fake followed by a back fist

ATTACK BY TRAPPING: Here is where you execute a trapping action on your opponent to immobilize them for your follow up attack. A trap could also be the attack itself.

Example of Attack By Trapping - Leg check, hand check, fllow up reverse punch

Example of trapping the arm and follow up reverse punch. This photo was taken at the 1973 National Black Belt Championships in Albuquerque, New Mexico. This phot was first published in Professional Karate Magazine.

ATTACK BY DRAWING: This is where you draw your opponent into an attack by one of three ways: 1) *Bait* - you leave an area open for them to attack and then hit them as or after they come in. 2) *Push* - you use constant forward pressure to get your opponent jumpy so that they will attack you out of desperation, a "keep away" action and then you key off that motion to throw your attack. 3) *Pull* - you move slightly away again and again until your opponent attacks you or tries to chase you down and then you hit them as they come in.

Example of baiting your opponent into throwing a reverse punch from too far away and into your counter

Example of using push to goad your opponent into prematurely attacking and running into your reverse punch

In this example, you constantly pump your opponent to make him jumpy so that he attacks prematurely. As he attacks, you pull away just enough for him to miss and you can hit him in the opening.

Example of using pull to goad your opponent into chasing you right into your attack

Following the lines on the floor, you see that you creep back, one step at a time, and your opponent readjusts the range by taking a step forward. You do this a couple of times on an impatient opponent and he'll get tired of it and take off on you moreso out of frustration than a well planned atack. Then you over extend him and counter punch (illustrated) or counter kick.

This is the exact strategy I used in my match with Keith Vitali when I won over him at the 1979 Mid-America Diamond Nationals.

Clashing with Keith Vitali in our lightweight title match. It was a close one that was finally decided in overtime.

DEFENSIVE APPROACHES:

HIT AS THE OPPONENT CHANGES: Whenever they change (shift their stance, drop an arm, look at a different area, etc.) you attack. I put this in the defense category because you are moving off of your opponent's action rather than setting your opponent up and initiating your own.

Example of hitting as your opponent changes - stance change in this illustration

HIT AS THE RANGES CROSS: You move forward as they move forward and hit them at mid distance.

Example of Hit As The Ranges Cross
Notice how much distance I need to cover to hit my opponent with a reverse punch

He steps in and hits me as I start to cover distance. This way he hits me in mid-move.

HOLD YOUR POSITION AND HIT: You hold your ground and hit them as they come at you.

Example of Holding Your Position and countering a back fist with a side kick

Example of Holding Your Position and countering a back fist with a reverse punch

SIMULTANEOUS BLOCK AND COUNTER: You block their attack and hit them back in the same move.

Example of a Simultaneous Block and Hit against a back fist

BLOCK AND COUNTER: You block their attack and counter attack them in a 1-2 action.

Example of Blocking a front kick and Countering with a reverse punch

EVADE AND COUNTER: You move the target they are hitting at out of the way of the attack and then hit them back. EVADE: You move away from their attack without counter attacking.

Example of Evading a side kick and Countering with a back fist

One of the main rules for fighting that I go by is THE SITUATION DICTATES THE RESPONSE. Nothing has to be. What I mean by this is that there are no exact ways to respond to any given attack. The position you are in at the time you're attacked, your attitude, your surroundings, etc., all play in the overall situation that is occurring. All of those factors will add into how you are going to respond at that moment. Five minutes later you may be attacked in the same fashion and you might have a totally different response.

Offensive Approach Counters

What I am going to outline here are what I feel to be the best objective counters to each approaches themselves, which action of one will best counter the action of another.

DIRECT ATTACK can be countered by any of the defensive approaches.

Example of a Direct Attack (back fist) countered by Hit As The Ranges Cross

ATTACK BY COMBINATION countered by *Hit as the ranges cross*; stop it before it gains any momentum or *evade and counter*; get out of the way and counter.

Example of Evade and Counter (side step and side kick) against Attack By Combination

INDIRECT ATTACK countered by *hit as the ranges cross*, attack as they are trying to set up, *hold and hit*; as their first action will be a fake or attention getter you can just hold your position and hit them as they set up, *evade*; frustrate them by simply moving out of range.

Example of using Hit As The Ranges Cross (step in and hit) against an Indirect Attack (hip fake)

Example of using Hold Your Position and Hit (side kick) to counter an Indirect Attack (fake punch - backfist)

Executing a pick off side kick against Bob Heuer of Longview, Washington.

ATTACK BY TRAPPING can be countered by *evade and counter/evade*; move away as they try to immobilize you, *hold and hit*; hit them as they try to grab you, *simultaneous block and counter*; deflect their grab and hit them at the same time.

Example of Attack By Trapping countered by Evade And Hit - pull the hand away from the trap

Example of Attack By Trapping countered by Hold Your Position And Hit - use his push to fire your punch

Example of Attack By Trapping being countered by Simultaneous Block And Counter

ATTACK BY DRAWING can be countered by *evade*; the main function of that approach is to draw you into attacking them, so instead of attacking you move away.

Example of Attack By Drawing being countered by Evade - he baits you and you step away

One similarity to the defensive styles of Keith Vitali and me is that often we took to the air for counter strikes. As you can see in this photo, it netted neither of us any result.

Defensive Approach Counters

HIT AS THE OPPONENT CHANGES can be countered by *attack by drawing*: as they are cueing on a change, you set them up with a specific type of change that will draw them right into your attack.

Example of Hit As Your Opponent Changes being countered by Evade And Counter

For someone known for a backfist, I landed a few reverse punches as well.

Example of Hit As Your Opponent Changes being countered by Indirect Attack

Fake the punch causing your opponent to fire prematurely. Follow up with a punch of your own.

Firing off a back fist strike at the 1971 Seattle Open Karate Championships. Before the use of hand and foot pads, we used to tape our hands to make our strikes more visible to the judges.

HIT AS THE RANGES CROSS can be countered by *indirect attack*; here you use broken rhythm or a fake as a false lead and as they cross the range, you hit them, *attack by drawing*; use Push, (stated earlier in this section) to draw them into your attack.

Example of Hit As The Ranges Cross countered by Indirect Attack - "Broken Rhythm From Japan" technique

In the above example, you take a short step forward and fake a reverse punch. Your opponent moves in to meet you in the middle. Since you took a shorter step than usual, his punch meets air. You move in on the recovery of his punch and hit him. This way you use his aggressive action against him to your advantage.

HOLD YOUR POSITION AND HIT can be countered by *direct attack*; you time and cross the range explosively enough to hit them before they hit, *indirect attack* for the same reasons as Hit as the Ranges Cross.

Example of countering Hold Your Position and Hit with a direct attack. Here you take a short lead step, thereby staying out of range as he hits. Follow up with a round kick to the head.

An example of the above technique against Mark Kaliciak of Canada.

Example of Hold Your Position And Hit countered by Indirect Attack (hip fake - round kick)

SIMULTANEOUS BLOCK AND COUNTER and **BLOCK AND COUNTER** can be countered by *indirect attack*; you fake something for them to block and hit them as they block or when they pause as they see that nothing is coming at them.

Example of using Indirect Attack to counter Block And Counter. He goes for the fake kick, you punch him.

EVADE AND COUNTER and EVADE countered by *direct attack*; here you have to make sure that you have them cornered before you attack. *Attack by trapping*; very often an opponent will be cueing off a hit or a kick type of attack so a grab or a tackle will possibly get by them. Also, as in Direct Attack, make sure that you have them cornered.

Example of using Attack By Trapping to counter Evade And Hit. He side steps and sets up to counter with a back fist. You check his arm and fire off a reverse punch.

When your opponent is slow to react (has a slow reaction time), you can use pretty much what you choose on them. Look to see if they have a fast reaction or not. If they have fast reaction timing, then your choice of offensive or defensive approaches will have to be chosen wisely.

Throw a few fakes to determine your opponent's reaction timing. Keep in mind that the more fatigued your opponent gets, the slower their reaction time so this may become a factor in a match.

CONFRONTING DRILL TO AID YOUR SPARRING

I started working with my white belts on this confront drill back in 1981 and had great success with it and have ever since. I am going to include it in this material for your use. The exercises went in this order: 1) 5 punch drill - no blocking, get hit (lightly) with each one. 2) 5 punch drill - block any two, get hit with three. 3) Light sparring - first no Blocking and then later, choose which attacks you wish to block and which you intend to get hit with. On the surface, the last one sounds absurd, "Choose the shots I'm going to eat?! I don't want to eat any of them!" Let's take a closer look, step by step.

Step 1. (Note: my original 5 punch drill is a blocking development exercise.)
Confronting a series of attacks and being able to have *(accept)* them come at you and land. Here you are making it all right for an attack to come in and hit you, rather than resisting it. Resistance will absolutely do nothing to help you handle it. Acceptance is the key. Resistance here is placed in the context of *mentally* resisting the attacks very existence or resisting the consequences of it hitting you. This manifests itself in flinching, closing your eyes, etc. When you can accept the fact that the opponent's attack is coming in at you and can do that with an air of calm, that leads to being able to handle it.

Step 2. Here you are choosing how you are going to get hit and when. An interesting phenomenon occurs when you choose what you are going to get hit with. You are actually placing attention on every maneuver or attack your opponent does because you are going to let this one hit you and decide to handle that one and so on. What is happening here? "All of a sudden" nothing is escaping your surveillance, your radar is on and you're catching it all. When you pick and choose, your confront has to come up enough to be able to pick and choose in the first place. This is better than having something come at you and flinching or ducking in fear.

Step 3. This is doing step 2 in sparring. Usually the goal of fighting or competition is "I hit you - you don't hit me." This is fine, except it is usually set up on a positive-negative reward validation basis. You hit them and you feel great. You get hit and you don't feel so great. Under this system every time you get hit, you just blew it. Bang - instant invalidation - instant put down.

There is another aspect of this. This is the concept of being "at cause" over what is happening in sparring. If you use the "I hit you - you don't hit me" validation goal of sparring, when you successfully hit and keep from getting hit, you are in command of the situation, you are at cause. When they hit you, you lost your being at cause for that moment. The result of that is either you rise to the occasion or you tighten up, get frustrated, or try too hard. Or even mentally concede the match ("they're better than me... to "I'm having an off night").

What happened is that under the standards you set up, you stopped being at cause over what was happening when you got hit. It goes through a downward spiral of action somewhat like this: I didn't want that to happen, they are now at cause and not me. I have got to get it back! And so on.

Now if you allow the other person to hit you, you are not only being at cause when you hit someone, but also when you get hit. When you allow them to hit you, this takes your resistance to their attacks and throws it out the window. You are freeing up the space between yourself and your opponent and in doing so, you are becoming more at cause over the situation.

When you can allow yourself to be hit by another, you are taking off all the negative significances attached to their attack. This is a way of mentally handling an attack. Give it freedom do not resist its existence. Allow it to come at you. When you can allow it to be, to exist, to fly at you with destructive force and not flinch, duck or hide, then you can do whatever you want with it without being tensed. Block it, let it hit you; let it fall short, anything. Freeing their attack up will free you up. Resist their attack and that resistance will tighten you.

When you are at the point of your training where you feel relaxed about which ones you are going to handle and which ones you're going to let land, then you're ready to apply it in sparring. What you want to do is to allow your opponent to throw whatever they wish and you handle it, not allowing it to land. This is just like before you started this exercise but with a major difference. You are no longer resisting your opponent's actions but are operation simultaneously with, and independent of them. The end result of this will be akin to what Bruce Lee meant when he said that your technique will be my technique.

It is all mental training. It is all confront training. The first step is to decide what will hit you. Allowing it to hit is allowing it to exist. When you can allow it to exist, then you can do with it as you please. I don't advocate allowing taking a full power side kick in the ribs but I fully advocate letting your opponent throw one. Again, if you don't resist it your mind will not lock up in the resistance and you'll be able to handle it easily.

When teaching this one thing I stress heavily is to go very light on the amount of impact in the beginning and then build it up in small gradient amounts. I find the one common feeling among my students when they are training at this is that the attack becomes less scary and easier to deal with. This is basically written data to accompany experience. Do steps 1, 2, and 3 and you will see what I mean. If you try to conceptually understand this without experiencing it, you will not get anywhere near the full benefit or overall understanding. As for the feeling of it being absurd or unworkable, you'll have to trust me on this one. I have had 100% success when I have taught it whether to students or in seminars.

NOTE: There is one way to cheat on this exercise and that is to choose which attack to get hit with in numerical sequence rather than choose the attack itself. "I'm going to get hit with numbers 1 and 3." and then grit your teeth when numbers 1 and 3 come along. That doesn't accomplish a thing. Spot the attack itself, choose to get hit with it, and watch it hit you. To do this exercise right, watch every attack.

So, go through steps 1-3 at an easy to deal with speed. As with everything else, do it at the proper gradient level FOR YOU. What is your proper gradient level? What can you handle easily? Start there. Then make it a little bit tougher. Stay at that level until it is easy to handle and then make it a little bit tougher again, and so on. This holds true for the speed of the attack and the degree of impact.

A common occurrence that happens when you are working on too high of a gradient level is speeding up to counter the frustration of being in over your head. When you are finding this happening, get your partner to slow down so that you can work to a point where you can handle the level you are working for. You ever wonder why white belts fight as if their clothes are on fire? This is the reason why.

DEFENSIVE SET UP

I have been regarded as one of the premier defensive fighters ever to compete on the open circuit. I've gotten a lot of *"How do you keep from being hit with a...?"* questions so I thought I'd outline how I set myself up defensively and my viewpoints behind what I do.

I fight out of a defensive frame of mind. In my opinion anybody can learn how to hit without a whole lot of training. Keeping from getting hit is a whole different matter and is what separates the men from the boys (and women from the girls). Most fighters are offensively minded. Usually their defensive skills come under the heading of what I call "barricading the fort." This is like in the western movies where the army is holed up in a fort and they don't start shooting until the Indians are climbing the walls.

This is an introverted, "handle it as it comes at you" type of thinking. You have to remember that they are firing at you while you are waiting for them to get close. You can fire on them as them come near but what do you do if they have superior fire power? I prefer to use positioning to cut off most of my opponent's options way before he ever begins to throw an attack. This is like throwing up roadblocks and detours (through the swamp) so he doesn't have a good, clear route to the fort. You get the idea? The other guy doesn't know where to begin. There are several tools I use to do this.

1. RANGE. I keep my opponent either where he can't hit me or I get too close to him for his comfort.

2. POSITIONAL SET UP. Refer to that chapter in Section One of this book.

3. PLACEMENT OF SELF (including footwork). How can I stand and how can I place my hands and arms so that my opponent has no targets or has to attack in the areas I choose? Am I set up so that I am in the way of his favorite techniques?

4. PRIOR OBSERVATION. If I've seen him before and what he did well and so forth, I can use that knowledge to set myself up accordingly. If I haven't, I'll go by 1-3 above.

Here are two factors that play heavily into this. You need to be able to kick and punch with both sides, not just the right or left. A position you use to limit your opponent will, to some degree, cut out some of your options too. Therefore, you will need the use of both your hands and both your feet. Plus, if you can hit with both limbs at will, you will be able to fire your attack from any position, offensive or defensive, rather than have only one position to hit from.

The other factor is to be brutally honest with yourself about your reaction speed. Is your reaction time quick or not? Do you get hit with sudden moves or do you handle them without getting hit? If your reaction speed isn't too quick, don't worry about it. Just increase the distance between you and your opponent and monitor more closely. I have different reaction speeds on different nights and I do the above to fix it.

Go over Monitoring in this section and Positional Set Up in section 1 to compliment this chapter and you'll see where I'm coming from better.

Ambidexterity is a key principle I teach. I am naturally right sided but have trained my left side as well.

RESPONSIBILITY

This is a letter that I gave to my students several years ago. Responsibility is a word that has somewhat bad connotations in this days society. It is usually lumped in with the concepts of taking the blame or paying the penalty for a wrong done. Being responsible is merely assuming being the cause point for all actions taken. When you can say to yourself "I am the cause for all that I do" you are beginning to take responsibility. It is not so hard to do.

Where this plays a huge part in your growth in karate is that when you realize that you will progress in a parallel line to the degree that you assume responsibility for your own progression, you will be in command of how fast you will become skilled. Then you can determine just how you wish to progress-if you wish to take your time or want to blaze along. In the long run, it is up to you. As your instructor, I feel that whatever rate of progression that suits your interest level is fine, as long as there is a steady rate of progression.

When thinking about your speed of progress, keep in mind that as your instructor, I can guide you toward the path but you have to do the walking. I can teach but you have to train. The attainment of skill is solely on your shoulders. It is your responsibility and your win when you progress. Your rewards come from your efforts. I can show you how but only you can make you do.

DIRECTIONAL FORCE

Along with Positional Set Up, this will be helpful in spotting what your opponent is throwing at you.

When you think about any particular attack, you'll find that it has three parts to it:
1. Point of origin, where it starts from.
2. Travel route, the route it takes getting from one spot to another.
3. Point of destination, where it hits or intends to hit. This is standard data for all of you who have studied the Monitoring section of my first book. Let us now take a look at, not specific attacks, but the overview of attacks.

Many methods of teaching will insist upon the difference between techniques because of the striking surface. For example: straight punch, one knuckle punch, palm heel punch, and the eye spear are all different attacks ... or are they? They all travel at you from point of origin, through the same route of travel though they have different striking surfaces. They can all be lumped under the same directional force category of "straight" can't they?

Examples of directionally "straight" attacks- straight punch, palm punch and eye spear

Notice that ridge hand and hook punch are directionally the same

Notice that round kick and hook kick are directionally curved actions

Many instructors place heavy emphasis on this concept and my Modern Arnis instructor, Remy Presas, also placed emphasis on it. The spotting of attacks as directional force types is not unique to karate and kung fu but applies to other arts as well. Prior to teaching this concept, I prefer to have my students develop their monitoring skills first and then apply this concept of spotting directional force attack types at green belt. I find it blends very well at this level and fits in with my teaching. When monitoring skills become senior to thinking then it really doesn't matter what the striking surface is.

Now let me get to specifics and examples. You can get quite complicated with all the potential angles of travel an attack can take. Therefore, in order to simplify, an attack can come at you from a 90-degree angle and a 45-degree angle. A 90-degree angle is straight - straight up and down and straight to the right and left, and straight at you. A 45-degree angle is halfway between the previously mentioned points. 90-degree angles are the points of the compass N, E, W, S. 45-degree angles are the points of the compass SE, SW, NE, NW. It is that simple.

Now you have circular and straight attack types. These are easy to recognize since the attacks are from one point of the compass to another. Things really begin to simplify when you look attacks from this viewpoint. Consider this - hook kick and round kick are the same in terms of directional force. So are the side kick and straight punch. Good martial arts are based on simplicity and this is another method of simplification.

RECOGNITION

A student's early training and a lot of what is written in my first book deals with thinking and how to think while sparring. Thinking is merely step one. It takes a lot to get a person to what they are doing. Much of society training is based on being able to go on automatic and doing things by rote. Go home and watch television and see how easy it is to get "glued to the box." That is a nice way of describing going on automatic.

To think about something is to consciously put attention into an area. Several columns in my first book describe going on automatic (*Circuits/Habit Patterns*) and how to think (*Objective Analysis in Sparring, How To Think While Sparring*). Thinking is stage one. You are beginning to wake up.

Recognition is the next step. RECOGNITION IS SENIOR TO THINKING. In order to recognize, you have to be awake and aware of what is happening in your own space and that includes the physical body of your opponent. You have all this information you have been learning about and are getting to know. When your knowledge and ability to confront come up, your ability to recognize will come up with it.

Example of recognizing. I spot Dexter Brooks launching a punch and I kick to counter.

The ability to instantly recognize an attack and its intention is very much an above average skill. Recognition is a form of knowing. You don't have to check the data banks in order to determine what the attack is and how to handle it. Think about it. How do you know when you know something? When you know. Do you know what your middle name is? Do you know or do you have to check your birth certificate to make sure?

That is the basic idea. When you recognize something, you are consciously aware of it. It's not automatic. It just operates faster than thought process. It's instant knowing.

HOW TO DEVELOP NEW VIEWPOINTS AND SKILLS

I came across this in class one night. We were working on a specific viewpoint and my students were having limited success working it in their sparring. So, I told them to really get into to drill and so forth. Then one of my students said to me that he was having trouble fitting it in with his sparring. That immediately told me what the problem was. He was trying to fit it in with his sparring. That is going about it backwards. When you are trying out a new approach, don't try to fit it in with your repertoire, fit your repertoire around the new approach. You should work everything around the new viewpoint instead of the other way around.

You have in your repertoire all sorts of techniques that you feel comfortable with. When you try out something new, all these other things will get in the way of the new approach if you try to fit the new approach in to the already comfortable actions. Comfortable over uncomfortable, successful over unproven actions - it's natural to stick with things that feel good or workable. The idea here is to begin operating out of the new viewpoint totally and those things that work well with it, keep. Those that don't, discard them.

Here's a good example of developing new skills. I am naturally right handed. I worked long and hard to develop my left leg so that I could end up throwing left leg kicks, as pictured above.

Here is an example: Let's say that you fight out of Horse Stance and feel comfortable with back fist and side kick. You need to develop your Front Stance fighting ability. Instead of fitting your Front Stance *into your normal routine*, switch to Front Stance and make Front Stance your routine. Now, if side kick doesn't fit in with your new routine, then don't try to use it. If the back fist does work, keep it.

Do you see? You fit your repertoire of techniques around the new approach, not fit the new approach in your repertoire. Once the new approach feels more natural, then it will naturally become part of your overall repertoire.

DIRECTIONAL FOCUS

The idea of directional focus is a combination of monitoring, preparedness and forward intention. You want to direct your attention and intention directly toward your opponent.

Monitoring wise, any time you get caught unaware or off guard, your focus was not there, period. At all times you want to focus on your opponent so that you will know what they are doing and how they are positioned. Every great fighter knew exactly where their opponent was.

Attack wise, you can direct your focus through your attacking agents - the hands and feet. Point them and keep them on your opponent at all times in whatever position they need to be in prior to the attack. For example, don't try to throw a straight punch when your arm is set up for a back fist. Throw the back fist or else change your position for the punch. This way you are aligned with your opponent. Try to shoot a target without aiming the gun directly at it. You will miss. The same holds true with an attack.

You focus your entry footwork the same way you focus your attacking agents, right at your opponent. This way you don't get tripped up on sloppy footwork or cut short your gap bridging. If you step from a front facing foot position, use the toes as your guide. From a side facing foot position, use the edge of your foot or heel to aim with. Use these points to direct your entry movement like the point of an arrow leading the shaft. Everything follows the point.

Intention wise, directional focus in your attitude will be the difference in any match. Your attitude should be in terms of, "This is what I'm going to do to you." A lot of fighters get caught up into "What are they going to throw at me?" Read back over the last two sentences and see the difference in the directional focus.

Joe Lewis (R) is considered to be one of the greatest karate fighters of all time. He is a prime example of what I call directional focus. Even in a posed photo after a seminar, look at his eyes. He means business.

This is from a conversation I had with Steve Fisher, 4 time Top Ten rated fighter.

D. A. "Well, he's pretty good."
S. F. "That means I'm going to beat his butt"
D. A. "What if he's better than you?"
S. F. "He's going to get it that much worse"
D. A. "I mean, he's #1."
S. F. "He's had it!"

You can read this and feel who is shooting the arrows and is getting stuck.

Everything, attitude wise, is in terms of what I'm going to do to you. You attack with that attitude, you defend with that attitude, and you even run away with that attitude. Japanese styles of karate are known for being direct. Take a look at the hand position of a Japanese stylist. The positioning may not be optimum for defense but they have both hands aimed right at you with the intention of spearing you with a punch that is going to send you to the moon. THAT'S DIRECTIONAL FOCUS! Your mind is a shotgun with both barrels aimed.

Having been a defensive fighter for many years, I have found that you can move backward with your intention, focus and perception still being forward. Most people, when on the defensive, their focus goes behind them. When you back up but still look for openings, your focus is still forward.

Always have your focus outwardly directed. Fight out the front door and not out the back.

THE FIRST STEPS TO LEARNING HOW TO TOURNAMENT FIGHT

Recently, I had undertaken a project consisting of getting white belts prepared for an upcoming tournament. What I was after was more of an understanding of what to expect and how to handle it rather than an immediate proficiency in all the aspects of tournament fighting. Here is the step-by-step breakdown of what I did:

1) Your opponent lets you score one technique.
2) You play give and take; you score one, then they score one, etc.
3) You block their attack and they let you score with the counter.
4) Play give and take using #3.
5) Your opponent moves at you, you hit them as they cross the range.
6) You play give and take with #5.
7) You are two points behind and there is only 10 seconds left.
8) You are two points ahead and there is 1 1/2 minutes left in the match.
9) The score is tied and the first point wins.

As you can see, this is a basic approach to give the student some reality of a tournament situation. The first six give the student some different ways of attacking and defending. The last three put them in the hot seat; when they are really behind, when they are really ahead, and when the match rides on a single point.

The main idea that I try to get them to apply is that a tournament match is a game of who gets whom first. The point that a judge or a referee will call is usually the one that looks the cleanest and the first one in. So, I usually work with the white belt on going in with one shot and making it really good. From there, I have them work on blocking their opponent's first attack and coming back with a good counter. After that, I get them to attack as their opponent begins to approach them, to get the jump on them. Then, it's heavy-duty attack on #7, protecting lead with #8, and making sure you are the first in on #9.

These first steps, I find, are all that are needed to acquaint a beginner with tournament fighting.

DOING AND TRYING

Frustration. How do you deal with it? Everybody has the problem of mentally beating themselves half to death to some degree or another. One of the consistent factors that has cropped up with every student I have taught in regards to frustration in learning has to do with the concept of "trying." When you "try", you are attempting something and that attempt includes the possibility of succeeding or failing.

Take a look at that. If you are trying to do a good side kick for twenty minutes and finally do a good one, you have spent twenty minutes doing one kick - the good one. Ask a student who is practicing a kick or punch. They usually think in terms of how many good techniques done. They'll say, "I've

done several real good ones." You asked them how many side kicks they have done in the last half hour. Gads, what a self put down! They just told you indirectly that most of the last half hour was wasted with the exception of a couple good kicks. Come on. They did more than five side kicks in that last half hour.

Talk to a weight lifter after an exercise period. Ask them what they did. They will tell you how much they lifted and how many times with each exercise. They were doing, not trying. When you look at the difference between doing and trying, you find that doing is far more positive minded. Instead of only doing two or three really good side kicks in the last half hour, how many side kicks did you do in the last half hour? Never mind that some were better than the others, how many did you do? 500 you say? Now look at that in terms of accomplishment. That you did 500 side kicks is quite an accomplishment.

Whenever training, it is most beneficial to look at the most positive aspect of it as you can. This way, you can accomplish something every training period. There are enough ways to be made to feel low out in this world without you mentally flogging yourself as well. Get into the frame of doing rather than trying. You'll feel much better.

MORE ON OPERATIONAL MODES

I went over Operational Modes in my first book, however, I have some additional information that didn't make it in time. An operational mode is the overall description of how your opponent fights. Whether they are aggressive or defensive is an operational mode. If they are aggressive, they will be prone to using offensive techniques, forward action, etc. They may have all sorts of different approaches to use but their overall mode of operation is aggressive. The same holds true with a defensive fighter. They can be typecast in this way.

Another category of operational mode you can look for is the type of energy your opponent displays. This I got from a kung fu practicing friend of mine, Doug Bailey. Your opponent can fight out of three energy types: *explosive energy*; a *pressuring, scattered energy*, and a *lulling energy*.

The *explosive energy* is when your opponent takes off with a sudden quickness, a blast off. A good way to look at this fighter is that he is wound up tight, just waiting to happen. Give him the opening or push him too hard and he explodes towards you, full speed, full commitment.

Example of explosive energy

The *broken rhythmic, pressure type of energy* is like radio static, a non-flowing, jerky, unbalancing, unnerving action. This guy scatters his opponent's energy by using a lot of false leads coupled with heavy forward pressure intention. He's looking for the scattered or unnerved reaction before he moves in to score.

The *lulling energy* is a drifting, floating action. Nothing really sets you off or unbalances you but they get in close enough to hit you before you can react. An interesting effect of the lulling energy fighter is while the explosive or broken rhythm fighter's energy can actually raise their opponent's energy level the lull fighter can lower their opponents energy level by their relaxed demeanor. Then when the energy drops, they tag them.

Which type of fighter are you? What operational mode do you operate out of? Are you aggressive or defensive? What kind of energy do you display and what type of fighters do you have trouble with? The answers to these questions you can best answer as you work on spotting you and your opponent. Check this out and you will be able to read your opponent that much better.

DESIRE

One thing I wanted to go over at the close of this section is that I can coach you (via this book) on all the techniques and strategies in the world but there is one thing that I can't give you. That is desire. That is the one thing that has to come solely from you. This is what takes the average karate player and makes a champion out of them. I've seen mediocre karate players win far more than I expected just because they wanted to win bad enough. I've also seen some of the most talented karate players do nothing for lack of desire.

Desire is the common denominator of all great champions whether they are in karate or in some other sport. It isn't strategy, physical ability, or who your instructor is although they may play a part in the overall result. It is the desire to overcome anything that may come in the way of your becoming a champion. That means overcoming a five point deficit, moving to another location in order to work with better people, putting in an extra hour every night to work on your reverse punch. That is desire. If you aren't doing everything possible to achieve your goals, then you don't want it bad enough.

Here's how badly I wanted it.

How badly do you want it? That is the question. I personally came from a region where nothing was happening in the way of national competition at the time. We had local tournaments but nothing that attracted any nationally known competitors. So, went out on the road and spent a lot of money going to outside tournaments so that I could get the experience I needed to become better at the game. I asked everybody a ton of questions, watched everybody warm up and fight, listened in on other people's conversations, anything that I could do in order to take something home with me to work on.

It paid off. In 1972 I got my first national rating and was on my way to become the first fighter from the Pacific Northwest to be rated in the Top Ten ever. All of this happened because I wanted it more than anything else. I went for it with all systems go.

In 1990 I competed in the Seattle Goodwill Games Karate tournament. Dianetics was one of the sponsors of the Goodwill Games and I have been associated with Dianetics since 1982. I hadn't planned on competing but at the last moment I was needed. So, with less than a month to prepare, I went for it. Experience paid off but it wouldn't have if not for the desire. I came away winning two gold medals, one in the 80 kilogram division and the other in the team competition. Oh yeah, I was 37 years old at the time.

There is an old song by the pop group Chicago, which had a verse that truly summed it up for me. The song was "Saturday in the Park" and the verse goes *"...if you want it, really want it..."* That says it better than anything else I can say I've heard.

When it comes to winning, you have to want it so bad that you are willing to undergo any type of training to get better. The thought of losing should start your eyeballs vibrating, your socks unraveling, and the alarm clocks ringing. This way, when you are down by a point or two, you will not give up until the timekeeper calls time and the chief referee stops the match. That is desire and this is what you need to become a champion.

Example of desire. In 1974, Pete Rabino (Arizona), Allen Miller (Virginia), Roy Kurban (Texas), Jerry Piddington (California) and I (Oregon) got together to form the "Queen Mary" team and competed at the International Karate Championships in Long Beach, California. We were all regionally or nationally rated fighters getting together on a whim. I was the anchor man for the team. We were tied going into the last match. I ended up winning the match and the team title by 1 point. I fought a very fast and very game "Hotdog" Harvey who gave me nothing and made me work for every point I got. Team photo above right.

AFTERWORD

This section has not much to do with the rest of the book but is more of my just sitting down and talking with you through these pages. A lot has happened in the number of years between books, both in occurrences and in my own viewpoint concerning the game of competition and the martial arts overall.

This first thing is a funny one. The book you are now reading is, in a way, my third book. I finished the rough draft of my second book and then lost the blasted thing. I couldn't find it anywhere. Actually, when I had finished it, I was rather unsatisfied with it anyway. It seemed like a rehash of my first book. So, I began working on what became this book, starting totally new. I finished the first rough draft of this book and then guess what. Yep. I found the other one. I compared the first rough draft to the second and added the portions I liked from the original first draft and came up with the book you have in your hand now.

Super Dan's Tips To Refereeing

Over the number years, I have had several wonderful honors bestowed upon me. One was being selected by several fighters as one of the Top Ten fighters of all time. Karate Illustrated magazine had run a poll of the top tournament players over the years and when the votes were counted up, I had made several of the lists.

Later in the year, there was a referees rating and I was rated the 5th in the nation. This was especially validating because I try to play totally fair when I referee. These are several things I do to make sure that I am the best official I can be.

I sure liked this move. It's illegal now. Oh well.

1. I don't call what I can't see. This is especially tough when you know something landed but you didn't actually see it hit.

2. I never talk down to a fighter. One of the worst things you can do while being the center referee is to talk down to a fighter. Maintain control in the ring at all times but respect the fighters at the same time.

3. I make sure I know the rules inside and out and I carry a copy of the rules when I officiate.

4. I never hesitate to penalize a fighter for an infraction of the rules.

5. I don't let any fighter buffalo me with psyche games or sympathy ploys. I used to pull all of the tricks and the referees when I competed so I know most all of the tricks. The only difference is that I don't let them get away with that on me.

6. I don't play favorites. Whoever scores gets the point.

7. I try to keep a sense of humor with me at all times (I used to violate that one all the time.). There are a lot of funny things that happen in the ring and I enjoy them all. Plus, it keeps the fighters from worrying about the "hard ass" official and lets them get on with the match.

8. I acknowledge when I blow a call or when I've misquoted the rules. It happens. For me, the worst thing to do is try to bluff and bluster my way through a mistake. I let the fighter know I blew it. Competitors like honesty in an official.

One of the things that I feel makes me a good official is that I competed nationally for so long that I have a good idea of what a point is and how to treat a competitor. A competitor just wants an even break. They want the officials to be competent and fair and that's all. I've had competitors come up to me after they had lost and tell me that I was the best referee they had ever seen because I was fair. That's all the competitor wants, just a fair shake. When the rating came through, I knew I had done my job well.

Is There Anything New Out There?

One of the things which never ceases to amaze me in the martial arts is that there is really nothing new out there. Several instances strike me funny. One of them has to do with Suicide Stance.

I remember working on this over a period of several weeks and had finished completing a method of teaching it to my students. I felt quite pleased with my accomplishment, as I had never come across anything that dealt with facing that way. Well, a month or so after I did that research, a friend of mine told me of a seminar he went to given by William Cheung, the Wing Chun kung fu expert. He had gone over the same position, the same side stepping, etc. that I had been researching earlier.

This is the funniest one though. I had never read or seen or heard anywhere from any martial arts source that should look at the attacking agents, the hands and feet, when watching your opponent for a telegraph of their movement. I've been told to watch the shoulders or hips or eyes but never the hands. When I discovered about watching the attacking agents, my defensive ability and that of my students increased immediately.

Well, recently I came across a book by John Stevens called "The Sword of No Sword" about the life of a warrior, Yamaoka Tesshu. He translated this from Tesshu's writings (date approximately 1885), *"The two eye positions. After taking in the entire presence of the opponent, there are two* places one should set the eyes: either on the end of the opponent's sword or on the opponent's hands." Another major martial arts discovery down the drain. Actually I was overjoyed to find it. It certainly surprised me and validated me at the same time.

If You're Going To Be A Tournament Player...

I want to comment here on the tournament scene and the competitor. One of the things that every competitor should watch out for is using wins in tournaments as the means of self-validation of your skills. That road is a rocky road, even for the winners. The reason I mention this is because I was one who lived for the tournament win. When I won I was in seventh heaven and when I lost I hit the depths. The only thing I had in my favor was that I had the desire to become the best in my field. The result was that I became one of the best in my field.

But what of the karate player who lets the inconsistencies of the tournament game get them down? Tournament karate is, at the time of this writing, getting better but has a long way to go. What can a fighter do about it? One solution is to tell them if they can't stand the heat, stay out of the kitchen. That's rather negative, though. My advice for the discouraged competitor is if you want to be a champion, you'll need to put out 200% of your energies. And that's just to start with. You'll have to dig deep down and come up with that extra from somewhere to overcome the heartbreaks along the way. If you aren't willing to put that kind of commitment into the game, then don't use the game for your validation.

The current tournament game is very disorganized, the referees are less than uniformly competent, and who knows, you may live in region where you don't get much magazine coverage. If you aren't prepared to take that type of situation on, then play the tournament as a game. It's not worth the aggravation. It can be fun if you don't let it get out of proportion as far as its importance.

That may be an odd thing to hear coming out of me because, like I said before, I lived for the tournament win. The funny thing I found out when I started teaching more was that not many others do live for the tournament win like I did. Can you beat that? Anyway, if you want to be a tournament star, get in there and work, work, work and you'll get there. Otherwise, have fun with the game. That's what games are for, to have fun with.

Above photo - Portrait of a 15 year old starting out on a tournament karate career

Sport Karate All On It's Own

I heard a refreshing idea lately. None other than Hirokazu Kanazawa, the All Japan fighting champion of 1957-58 and highly rated Shotokan master, stated it. He mentioned in an article that he would like to see a sport karate evolve separately so that there would both be a sport karate and the martial art karate. I rather like that idea. Have the sport for those who are young and competitive and then have the martial art with the street aspect, discipline, culture, spiritual and mental training.

Above photos are me competing at the 1990 Goodwill Games where I won two Gold Medals

What Is A Martial Artist, Anyway?

This brings me to another area I would like to talk about and that is I find myself becoming more of a martial artist than a karate player as time goes on. Both Steve Fisher and Jack Farr, good friends of mine, said to me in 1980 at my third degree black belt test that I was a martial artist. I laughed at them and told them I was just a karate jock. They just smiled and said, "Wait." Later in Los Angeles, another friend told me the same thing. This was a few years later. Now as my competitive days are over, I am doing more martial arts than just karate. Let me explain.

My original concept of a martial artist was one of the Miyamoto Musashi type warriors, the bold fearless fighter who worked 18 hours a day perfecting his craft, leading a spartan existence. That certainly wasn't me. What I hadn't looked at was the concept of an artist.

An artist communicates through whatever medium they choose to be an artist in. A painter paints, a singer sings, an actor acts, and so forth. A martial artist communicates their love of the art through their practice and performance of it, whether in the ring or in private. They have a respect for the art. The funny thing is that during my period of gross irreverence for the formalities and exterior trappings of the martial arts, my love for karate never diminished. This is why, I believe, my desire for competition has waned.

This passion for my art has extended into other facets of the martial arts such as Modern Arnis, Small Circle Jujutsu, and Chinese soft styles. All of these would take another book to detail the whys and wherefores of my involvement. But this love for what I was doing and training at, this passion for the art is what makes me a martial artist.

This is what Steve and Jack saw. I'll be darned. I always thought of myself as being a "karate nut," a lifer. This puts a new perspective on things and helps the way I look at students. Which ones are there for the exercise and competition and which are for the art? Looking at it in this light I can be the best instructor for my students and can help them realize their goals far better, whatever they are.

The last thing I would like to include here is my own list of who I feel are the greats of tournament competition and the best matches I have ever seen. This list may cause a little controversy, as I have been off the tournament circuit since 1985 so one could suppose that this is a list of the Top Ten until then. Any subjective list will have its share of those who like it and those who don't. I have included both a men's and women's list of top fighters. This has to do with point competition because I haven't competed in full contact karate and therefore haven't seen or fought most of their fighters.

Super Dan's Picks For The Top Ten Male Karate Fighters Of All Time

1. **BILL "SUPERFOOT" WALLACE** - Everything that can be said about Bill has been said. Aside from his incredible kicking ability, the things that have impressed me about Bill have been his phenomenal balance, his timing, and his drive. Of all of the first P.K.A. full contact karate champions crowned in 1974, he was given the least chance to survive. He was the only one to retire undefeated.

2. **CHUCK NORRIS** - Now a movie star, back in 1966-68 Chuck won everything there was to win. He was the first diversified fighter - he used both hands and feet. Beneath his gentlemanly exterior was a drive to excel. His great sportsmanship attitude was a role model for many a champion to come.

3. **JOE LEWIS** - Joe is the universally acclaimed genius of American karate and was said to be ten years ahead of his time. Strong, rugged, and quick for his size (200 lbs.), he brought mobility and angular movement to the American karate scene. He was also the first conditioned athlete in point competition. Counting both point and full contact competition, Joe has probably the longest time span of any competitor in the top ranks.

4. **HOWARD JACKSON**, "The California Flash" - The best way I can describe Howard is this: Bill Wallace had the fastest kicks in karate. Howard's ability to bridge the gap was so explosive that he could move inside of Bill's kick. That's how fast he was. Outside of the ring, he was one of the nicest people you could meet. Inside the ring, he was one of the toughest. A knee injury in 1974 shortened what could've been truly one of the most awesome careers in sport karate ever

5. JEFF SMITH, "The D.C. Bomber" - I've seen Jeff fight a number of times and the one thing he had over all other fighters I've seen was confidence. He absolutely radiated an air of confidence. Considering that he shared his era with Bill Wallace and Howard Jackson, this was amazing. The other most notable points about him were his ability to spot other fighters weaknesses, his timing, and the fact he was just plain tough.

6. KEITH VITALI - Where Joe Lewis introduced footwork and angular movement to sport karate, Keith perfected it. Keith had the smoothest footwork of any player before and since his competitive career. The most interesting thing about Keith was that he was not explosively fast. He was technically exact and had deceptively sharp timing. His timing and ability to move at different angles made him very hard to hit and very frustrating to fight.

7. STEVE "NASTY" ANDERSON - Steve is the only fighter I have ever seen who has geared his entire fighting style to that of the sport game. He has been condemned by many for not being a rough and tumble fighter but when time has been called, more often than not, he is the winner. Steve has put to best use his natural assets, his reach and broken rhythm, and coupled them with a highly evasive defense and has turned them into a winning combination. He's probably the most unorthodox champion to have ever reigned.

8. DEMETRIUS "GREEK" HAVANIS - Known by his nickname, "Greek," he was one of the most awesome lightweights to have fought. Handicapped by his short height (5'5" tops), he turned himself into a veritable fighting machine. He was one of the few who could do just about any maneuver from either his left or right side. He would go to a tournament and warm up for 1-2 hours off to the side doing punching and kicking drills with weights on. I would never have believed it if I hadn't seen it for myself. "Greek" was in the middle of a promising full contact career when he lost his life in a plane wreck in 1982. Karate lost one of its finest then.

9. RON MARCHINI - Ron is overlooked by many newer competitors on the scene because he was never a flamboyant stylist. Strong basics and smart tactics were his stock in trade. He has beaten both Joe Lewis and Bill Wallace in point competition and has fought in Japan as well.

Matched against Hot Dog Harvey

10. STEVE MUHAMMED (formerly SANDERS) "Pops" is probably the most underrated fighter in American tournament karate history. Steve Muhammed had, bar none, the fastest hands in the game. The fact that he rarely traveled outside of the Los Angeles area prevented him from becoming a much greater star on the circuit. He is the only person I have ever seen who could fight with the rapid-fire combinations seen in a Kenpo form - in the ring successfully. I know from experience. I fought him and man, was he fast!

who I'd like to mention on the basis of their reputations. **MIKE WARREN** is said to have been the best technician to have ever fought. He didn't travel outside of the New York area much. **MIKE STONE** was the first national champion. He won all the tournaments in the 1963-64 era and then retired thereafter. He came out of retirement a couple of times to compete in special matches and then retired for good in 1970. **THOMAS LaPUPPET** was the first major east coast champion to make a splash on the national scene. He was a coach for the A.A.U. national karate team. **SKIPPER MULLINS** is said to have a right leg that is as every bit as good as Wallace's left leg. Skipper competed during the same time as Chuck Norris and was the top lightweight of that time.

One additional note: I have not included myself in this pick. This is not false humility or anything of the sort. I was one of the best in tournament competition history. In fact, I was honored in Houston, Texas in 2000 as one of the 50 most influential people in the forty year history of the sport. I did better than the vast majority of competitors, ever. The fighters I named, though, were the *best* of the best.

Super Dan's Pick Of The Top Women Fighters Of All Time

1. **LINDA DENLEY** - Linda is the combination of Martina Navratilova and Chris Evert Lloyd of karate. She has all of the athletic ability and strength of Martina and the longevity of Lloyd. She was the dominant force of women's karate competition for at least ten years. She is in a class all herself.

2. **ARLENE LIMAS** - If there is anybody who, in the long run, had a chance of eclipsing what Linda has established, it would've been Arlene. She was the only competition Linda had. Arlene is known for her kicking ability and ring strategy. She is truly the first sneaky woman fighter. She went onto be the first American to win a Gold Medal in the 1988 Olympics in Taekwondo.

3. **PHYLLIS EVETTS** - Plagued with bad knees, Phyllis, nevertheless, dominated the women's fighting scene along with Malia Dacascos during the late 1960's and early 1970's. She was from Texas and was tough from the word go.

3. **MALIA BERNAL** - I rated Malia a tie with Phyllis as she not only co-dominated the women's fighting, she also totally dominated the women's forms competition. Where Phyllis was a power fighter, Malia relied upon timing and accuracy to take her wins.

4. **BECKY CHAPMAN** - Becky received less publicity than she deserved because she competed during a time when the magazines were covering Linda Denley or concentrating on full contact karate beginnings. Becky was another pinpoint fighter, relying on accuracy rather than power.

5. **JOANNA NEEDHAM** - Joanna was a successful fighter in her region and then burst into the national limelight by snapping Linda Denley's 5-year winning streak at the Mid-America Diamond Nationals. She went on to be a dominant force in the women's ranks until she retired a couple of

years later.

6. **MIKIE ROWE** - In terms of publicity, Mikie was forever in the shadow of Malia Bernal. They were both from the kajukenbo system and Malia was the major winner of the two. Mikie was a sharp puncher and a tough competitor.

7. **PAULINE SHORT** - Pauline was the first woman fighter to compete outside of the Pacific Northwest region successfully in both forms and fighting. She was one of the pioneers of women's fighting competition in the 1960's. *(Pauline and I at the Internationals in 1972)*

8. **MARCIA HALL** - Marcia didn't compete in point fighting but I feel she deserves special recognition as she was the first American fighter, male or female, to win a gold medal in international taekwondo competition. In fact, she was the women's full contact taekwondo champion two years in a row. This was a full 10 years before the American Olympic team made a splash at the 1988 Seoul Olympics. I sparred with her and came away quite impressed. Although she didn't point fight I rate her as one of the best.

The Super Dan Pick Of The Best Matches I Have Ever Seen

I thought I'd include the best matches I have seen. I have competed as a black belt since 1970 and have seen a lot of black belt matches let alone competed in them. Here are my choices for the best.

STEVE FISHER in the team matches at the 1980 U-S Open Championships in St. Petersburg, Florida. Steve was a fighter who on his best days, had the most positive attitude of anybody. This day, Steve was unbeatable. He fought mostly heavyweights of the other teams and was a picture of precision and guts.

BOBBY TUCKER at the 1978 P.K.A. Nationals. This has a funny story to it. This tournament had to be the most drawn out tournament I have ever been to. The black belt fighting divisions began at 2:30 a.m. To top this off, the temperature was about 100 degrees in the gym with about 90% humidity. Needless to say, we were all dragging. Keith Vitali had bloodshot eyes, I was leading a group of jokers making snide comments about the tournament, Mike Genova was ready to go back to his camper where he had a cooler of ice cold beer waiting for him. That was the situation.

Then the black belt division began. Bobby Tucker ran through his opposition like a hot knife butter. I knew he was fast but nobody is that fast at 2:30 in the morning. He easily won the grand championship. I found out later that Bobby was a night person and was used to being up that late. He was awake when the rest of us were asleep.

JIMMY TABARES vs. Robert Harris at the 1980 Mid-America Diamond Nationals. Jimmy is about 5'2" or so and Robert is at least 6 feet tall. This match was amazing. Jimmy is a typical Texan and knows only one way to go - full speed ahead. Robert Harris is not the person to do that to. He hits like a mule and has some of the cockeyed timing I have ever seen. Jimmy was all over him like a mad pit bull. Every time the referee said go, Tabares was on him. He was ahead 4-0 when he hurt his knee trying to wrestle Robert down. He continued the match, winning it 4-2 and then had to withdraw.

JEFF SMITH vs. Everett Eddy at the US Championships in Dallas, Texas 1974. Jeff was a light heavyweight and in contention with Bill Wallace and Howard Jackson for the number one rating in the US. Everett was a heavyweight and was nicknamed the "Monster Man" because of his size. Jeff went toe to toe with him and even swept him out twice in a display of courage and hard fighting that impressed me. It was an amazing match.

STEVE SANDERS during the eliminations at the PAWAK tournament. This tournament was labeled the $64,000 tournament that nobody came to. The promoter figured that with this type of advertised prize money, a ton of competitors would show up and he could make the prize money from the entrance fees, which were around $50 per person (which was quite expensive back in 1974). Well, about 50 or so people showed up, there was only one weight division for the black belts and Steve creamed his opponents. He was there for the money and had trained to win. During the day he was unstoppable. Later, when the finalists found out that the promoter didn't have the money to pay them, Steve's spirits fell (along with everybody else's) and fought to half capacity in the finals. It was lucky for the promoter that the black belts decided to let him have his skin.

JOHN NATIVIDAD vs. **BENNY URQUIDEZ** at the International Karate Championships in 1974. John and Benny fought for the Grand Championship match in the highest scoring match ever. Between them they scored 25 points with John taking the match in overtime, 13-12.

These are the best matches I have ever seen in the 30 or so years I have been associated with tournament karate. I think it is amazing when athletes who are already great rise up for a performance that eclipses what they and others normally do. It makes for special moments.

One of the things I am proud of is to have been a part of the competition era between 1970-1985. To have fought against top fighters like Bill Wallace, Demetrius Havanis, Keith Vitali, Ray McCallum, Nasty Anderson, and others has been a blast. I don't believe there has been a more talented group of champions than those who were around in that 15 year period. My only regret is that I have never fought against Chuck Norris, Joe Lewis, or Skipper Mullins.

Top Ten players of 1979 at the Mid America Diamond Nationals (left to right) Keith Vitali, myself, Ray McCallum, Herb Nichols, John Longstreet, Mike Genova, Larry Kelley

The last word I want to put in here before I close is to keep in mind that if you really want to become a champion, you can. You'll have to put yourself to the task 200%…and that's just for starters. But there isn't a single one of you who can't do it if you want it bad enough. If I could do it, so can you! If you want to get in touch with me, you can reach me by sending a self addressed, stamped envelope to Dan Anderson Karate, PO Box 1463, Gresham, Oregon 97030 or e-mail me at www.dananderson karate.com and I will enjoy hearing from you.

Martial Arts Books by Dan Anderson

De-Fanging The Snake: A Guide To Modern Arnis Disarms

I recently purchased your Modern Arnis Disarms book, "Defanging the Snake". I have been impressed with your presentation of the material in a clear and consise manner. Finally, a martial arts book that delivers worthwhile material in a meaningful way. Thank you for taking the time and focusing your energy so that your teacher will live on for many generations yet to come in part due to your efforts. I have studied and taught Villabrille Kali and the Serrada Eskrima systems for more than twenty years and unfortunately neither system had much to offer in the way of disarms. That journey was left up to me to take on my own... Your teacher's books on Modern Arnis and now your book have contributed to my knowledge and on going research. Thank you.

Advanced Modern Arnis: A Road To Mastery

The long and short of it, it is clear to me that you are one of the select few who grasped the real genius of Professor's art, that ethereal flow.
- Brett Salafia

The pictures are clear and easy to follow. I have been to many of the camps, but nobody has a text that is this easy to follow. With all of the photos you can see a great amount of detail.
- Dugan Hoffmann

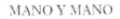

Mano y Mano: Weaponless Fighting Applications Of Modern Arnis

Master Bram Frank - This book fills in the gaps of his other books on Modern Arnis and the martial arts! If you ever wondered how Modern Arnis or Filipino Arts translates into empty hand, well this is the book for you.

Datu Shishir Inocalla - There are not too many authors of Filipino Martial arts empty hand techniques. I am glad that a Master Instructor and a martial arts champion such as Master Dan Anderson has taken this step to write "Mano y Mano - The Weaponless Fighting Applications Modern Arnis".

Fighting Tactics & Strategies

I received the book. Excellent. I find your explanations of techniques very readable and user-friendly. You provide enough detail so non-experts, such as myself, can really comprehend what you are explaining. Over my many years (although I think you have about 3-4 more years than me) I have seen instructors using some of these techniques, but I guess they were 'secret' because the exact 'how-to', step-by-step was not explained. I appreciate your sharing this knowledge.
Jim L.

I read your second book sparring book. It was awesome. Thanks for your help (directly or indirectly) on my sparring.
John Dickey

More titles available at www.danandersonkarate.com

Made in the USA
Las Vegas, NV
25 November 2024